Model
Everyday Letters
and Form Filling
3rd edition

If you want to know how ...

Quick Solutions to Common Errors in English
An A–Z guide to spelling, punctuation and grammar

The Little Book of Big Words
... and how to use them

Improve your Written English
*Master the essentials of grammar, punctuation and spelling
and write with greater confidence*

How to Write Essays
*A step-by-step guide for all levels,
with sample essays*

Writing Your Dissertation
*The bestselling guide to planning,
preparing and presenting first-class work*

Improve Your Punctuation and Grammar

Please send for a free copy of the latest catalogue:

How To Books
Spring Hill House, Spring Hill Road,
Begbroke, Oxford OX5 1RX
Tel: (01865) 375794. Fax: (01865) 379162.
info@howtobooks.co.uk
www.howtobooks.co.uk

Model
Everyday Letters
and Form Filling
3rd edition

*How to deal with everyday writing needs
without letting yourself down – with examples.*

Angela Burt

howtobooks

Published by How To Books Ltd
Spring Hill House, Spring Hill Road
Begbroke, Oxford OX5 1RX
Tel: (01865) 375794. Fax: (01865) 379162
info@howtobooks.co.uk
www.howtobooks.co.uk

How To Books greatly reduce the carbon footprint of their books by sourcing their typesetting and printing in the UK.

First published 2003
Second edition 2006
Third edition 2009

British Library Cataloguing in Publication Data.
A catalogue record for this book is available from the British Library

978 1 84528 316 2

Cover design by Mousemat Design Limited
Produced for How To Books by Deer Park Productions, Tavistock
Typeset by PDQ Typesetting, Newcastle-under-Lyme, Staffordshire
Printed and bound by Bell & Bain Ltd, Glasgow

NOTE: The material contained in this book is set out in good faith for general guidance and no liability can be accepted for loss or expense incurred as a result of relying in particular circumstances on statements made in the book. Laws and regulations are complex and liable to change, and readers should check the current position with the relevant authorities before making personal arrangements.

Contents

List of illustrations

Acknowledgements

I am indebted to my daughter, Anna Sendall, for permission to use the letter which appears on page 41.

Note from the Author

I hope that this book will offer practical help and guidance to all who lack confidence when faced with everyday writing tasks, whether it is having to reply to a formal wedding invitation, compiling a CV, or completing a job application form. Indeed, I have known a number of parents who become uncharacteristically nervous whenever they have to write to staff at their children's schools. I have borne them in mind by including a range of letters explaining a child's absence, apologising for homework not done and asking for leave of absence to go on a family holiday in term-time.

Everyday situations are discussed and sample responses provided in the belief that readers will just want to be shown what to do and then will be able to do it. They need the reassurance of straightforward explanations and instructive sample material.

Personal letters, business letters, job applications, formal invitations, classified advertisements and family announcements, minutes of meetings, agendas, press releases, posters and handbills are covered here. Useful spellings are listed in context as well as having dedicated space at the end. Punctuation is also dealt with in a section of its own: each punctuation mark is examined in turn and plenty of examples provided.

I hope this handbook will help you to write with confidence. That has been my aim at all times.

Angela Burt

Part One

- Postcards
- Personal letters

1

Postcards

There are two kinds of postcard:

a) the plain postcard which is used generally for business purposes

b) the picture postcard sent to friends, relations and colleagues when on holiday away from home.

PLAIN POSTCARDS

The plain postcard is, in effect, a short letter; on one side there is space for a brief message and, on the reverse, space for the recipient's name and address, and a stamp. (Remember, however, that, as no envelope is used, anyone can read your message while it is in transit.)

When might you use a plain postcard?

◆ You may be asked to enclose a self-addressed (and stamped) postcard with a job application if you want confirmation of the safe arrival of your documents. Such confirmation can be added very quickly to the message side before the postcard is posted back to you.

◆ Another occasion when you might prefer to use a postcard rather than to write a letter is when you are making a brief request (see Figure 1.3).

You have two layout styles to choose from: the fully blocked and the indented. Examples of each style are shown in Figures 1.1., 1.2., 1.3., and 1.4. Use whichever you are happier with.

POST CARD

THE ADDRESS TO BE WRITTEN ON THIS SIDE

Mr Alan Gibson
10 Mount View Avenue
EVELEIGH
Hants
PO3 9EW

Figure 1.1. The fully blocked layout

Note: a) Each line begins against an imaginary left-hand margin.
b) There is no punctuation at the end of each line.

POST CARD

THE ADDRESS TO BE WRITTEN ON THIS SIDE

Mr Alan Gibson,
10 Mount View Avenue,
EVELEIGH,
Hants,
PO3 9EW

Figure 1.2. The indented layout

Note: a) The address is sloped at an angle of 45°.
b) There is no punctuation in the postcode line but there is punctuation at the end of every other line. You may, if you wish, use a full stop instead of a comma after the county name.

103 Stakes Hill Road
DENSFORD
Merseyside
L45 2CE

1 June 200-

Dear Sir or Madam

I should very much like a copy of your catalogue of bedroom furniture, and a current price list.

Yours faithfully

Anne Evans

Figure 1.3. A postcard requesting information

The fully blocked layout

The example shown in Figure 1.3 shows a fully blocked layout. Note the relevant features:

- no punctuation at the end of the lines of the sender's address

- address written against an imaginary vertical line (= ranged left)

- no punctuation in the date (except relevant capital letters)

- no comma after the greeting (salutation): Dear Sir or Madam

- paragraphs not indented but blocked in line with the salutation

- no comma after the ending (the complimentary close): Yours faithfully

- the complimentary close and the signature ranged left in line with the text of the message.

An optional feature in a fully blocked layout is to position your address and the date on the left-hand side in line with what follows.

- Sometimes the organisers of competitions ask for entries to be submitted 'on a postcard, please', because postcards are of a standard size and can be easily filed and sorted.

◆ It can be convenient to use a plain postcard to send brief messages to friends.

The indented layout

The example that follows in Figure 1.4 shows an indented layout. Note the relevant features:

◆ address sloped at an angle of 45°, each line beginning slightly to the right of the starting point of the line above

◆ address punctuated traditionally

◆ commas used after the salutation and the complimentary close

◆ paragraphs indented to the same point (either directly in line with the comma at the end of the salutation or slightly to the left or right of it)

◆ complimentary close and signature in the right-hand half of the space available.

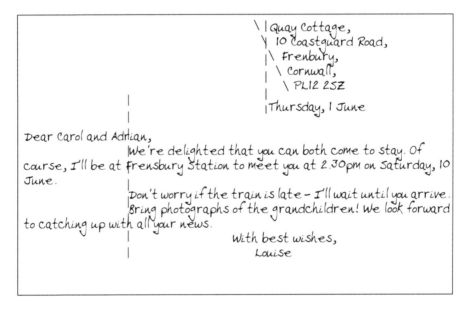

Figure 1.4. A postcard to friends confirming arrangements

If you use postcards regularly, you might like to consider treating yourself to printed ones. Your local printer will be able to show you several examples. One very attractive layout is when the address of the sender is printed at the top centre of the card. (You have the choice of writing in a fully blocked or indented layout thereafter.) A printed address on a postcard saves so much space (and time).

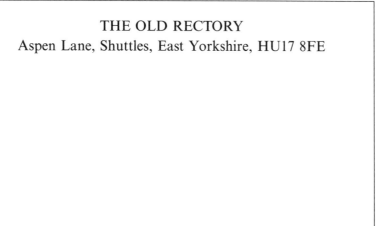

Figure 1.5. A postcard with printed address

PICTURE POSTCARDS

The 'picture' side of the postcard presents no problems, given a good selection of photographic views of your holiday resort. Picture postcards are chosen to share some of the pleasure of your holiday with those left behind, and you will want cards that show your venue in its best light or that will illustrate an aspect that you are particularly enjoying.

The challenge comes on the 'writing' side because there is really very little room. Picture postcards are usually larger than plain ones but if on average they measure 11 cm × 15 cm that means there is only a tiny space of 5½ cm × 7½ cm for the message. (Indeed there is sometimes less than this if there is a lengthy caption identifying the view shown on the other side.) The few words possible have to be chosen with care if we are to avoid clichés such as: 'Having a wonderful time. Wish you were here.' An additional challenge can be writing something different each time for those recipients who may see each other's cards!

In the example that follows, notice these features:

♦ no need for a salutation such as 'Dear Anne and Alan' (their names are just centimetres away to the right on the address half of the card. Space is limited!)

♦ no date needed (the postmark will indicate this)

♦ complimentary close optional (you possibly won't have room)

♦ relevant country added to the address on the right <u>before</u> the postcode. (This applies only if you are holidaying abroad.)

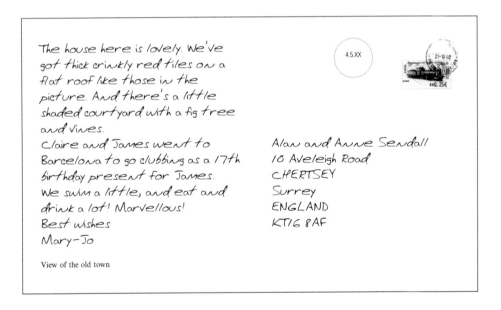

Figure 1.6. A holiday postcard

2

Personal Letters

When writing personal letters you have the choice of using either the fully blocked layout or the indented one, just as you have when writing business letters. These two layouts were described briefly in the previous section on postcards but we discuss them more fully here.

Each layout has its own simple conventions of paragraphing, positioning and punctuation.

FULLY BLOCKED LETTER LAYOUT

See Figure 2.1.

a) The address

◆ Notice how the writer's address is 'blocked'. Each new line of the address begins at exactly the same point.

◆ Notice also the 'open' punctuation. No full stops or commas are used above or below the main body of the letter in open punctuation. Care, however, must be taken with capital letters as always. Every word in an address usually begins with a capital letter, and the postal town and the postcode are written in block capitals.

◆ NB The writer's name should NEVER be written above the address at the head of the letter.

b) The date

◆ The date is spaced below the address and is aligned with it. See the dotted line as a guide.

◆ Notice 21 October and not 21st October. The fully blocked layout is a clear simple uncluttered one and –st, –nd, –rd are not used in dates.

◆ Never abbreviate the date to 21/10/0 – unless you are writing a very informal note.

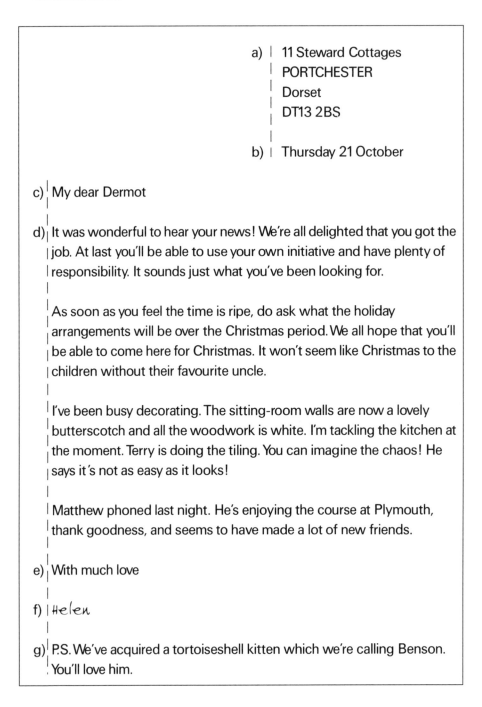

a) | 11 Steward Cottages
| PORTCHESTER
| Dorset
| DT13 2BS

b) | Thursday 21 October

c) | My dear Dermot

d) | It was wonderful to hear your news! We're all delighted that you got the job. At last you'll be able to use your own initiative and have plenty of responsibility. It sounds just what you've been looking for.

As soon as you feel the time is ripe, do ask what the holiday arrangements will be over the Christmas period. We all hope that you'll be able to come here for Christmas. It won't seem like Christmas to the children without their favourite uncle.

I've been busy decorating. The sitting-room walls are now a lovely butterscotch and all the woodwork is white. I'm tackling the kitchen at the moment. Terry is doing the tiling. You can imagine the chaos! He says it's not as easy as it looks!

Matthew phoned last night. He's enjoying the course at Plymouth, thank goodness, and seems to have made a lot of new friends.

e) | With much love

f) | Helen

g) | P.S. We've acquired a tortoiseshell kitten which we're calling Benson. You'll love him.

Figure 2.1. A fully blocked letter layout

♦ Often when writing a letter of this kind, the day of the week seems more relevant than the year. You can substitute 21 October 200- if you wish, however.

c) The greeting (or salutation)

♦ The punctuation is open. There is no comma after 'My dear Dermot' but capital letters are used appropriately.

♦ When writing to a friend or relation, you can, of course, choose any greeting which seems natural to you.

d) Paragraphing

♦ You will see that the paragraphs are 'blocked' and not indented. Paragraphs begin in line with the salutation (as does the rest of the letter).

♦ A space is left between the salutation and the first paragraph, between the last paragraph and the complimentary close, and between all paragraphs in between.

e) The ending (or complimentary close)

♦ The punctuation is open (no comma at end) but begins with an initial capital, as always.

♦ Notice the positioning of the complimentary close. It is on the left of the page, in line with the text above.

♦ In an informal letter to a well-loved friend or relation, use any complimentary close which seems appropriate, for example:
  – Yours affectionately
  – With best wishes
  – Sincerely yours
  – With love ever

f) The signature

♦ Notice the position on the left-hand side of the page in line with the complimentary close.

♦ No full stop is needed after the signature.

g) The postscript

◆ The word postscript comes from the Latin *postscriptum* and means 'after the writing has been finished'. A P.S. (postscript) at the foot of a letter to a friend is quite natural and appropriate. It is the written equivalent of the conversational 'Oh! I forgot to say...'. However, such an afterthought in a formal letter would be out of place. (A formal letter should be structured so carefully that if you forget an important point you have to write the letter again!)

◆ Notice the postscript in a fully blocked letter is aligned to the left.

◆ An additional afterthought would be marked P.P.S, and a third P.P.P.S. It's probably best to stop there!

FULLY BLOCKED ENVELOPE LAYOUT

The envelope layout (see Figure 2.2) can be fully blocked also.

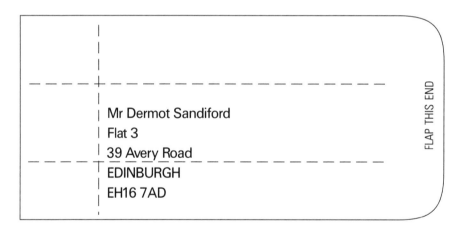

Figure 2.2. The fully blocked envelope

◆ Notice that the name and the address are 'blocked'. Each line begins against an imaginary vertical line.

◆ The punctuation is open.

◆ The postal town is written or typed in block capitals.

◆ Capital letters are used in the postcode. The two parts of the postcode are clearly spaced.

- Space has been left above the address for franking in the sorting process.

- Space has been left on the bottom of the envelope so that the last line of the address will not be covered when the envelope is carried upright on a conveyor belt during the electronic sorting process.

- Notice too that the flap is on the right-hand side (not the left). Some envelopes, of course, have the flap at the top.

INDENTED LETTER LAYOUT

Helen's letter to Dermot is shown now as an indented layout (Figure 2.3). Compare the two layouts, fully blocked and indented. You'll find that most business letters you receive will be fully blocked, and this format is becoming increasingly popular in handwritten, and typed, personal letters, but both layouts are equally acceptable. Choose whichever one is most comfortable for you and perfect it.

a) The address

- Notice the slope in the address. Each line begins a little to the right of the one above. You need to start the address at a convenient point to accommodate any long words that might be coming before the end like MORETONHAMPSTEAD or BUCKINGHAMSHIRE.

- As in the fully blocked layout, the postal town and the postcode are written with capital letters.

- Each line of the address is punctuated (except the postcode line). Some people like to use a full stop at the end of the line before the postcode; others prefer a comma. Either is acceptable.

- A comma after the house number is optional. The modern tendency is to omit it.

- It is always best to write words like 'Road' and 'Avenue' in full, except in very casual notes to friends, in both fully blocked and indented layouts. It is, however, quite acceptable to use recognised contractions for counties (Wilts., War., Oxon., Northants., Glos., Cambs., etc.).

NB Remember: never write your name above the address.

a) 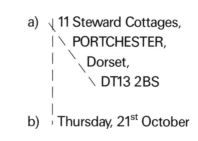11 Steward Cottages,
PORTCHESTER,
Dorset,
DT13 2BS

b) Thursday, 21st October

c) My dear Dermot,

d) It was wonderful to hear your news! We're all delighted that you got the job. At last you'll be able to use your own initiative and have plenty of responsibility. It sounds just what you've been looking for.

As soon as you feel the time is ripe, do ask what the holiday arrangements will be over the Christmas period. We all hope that you'll be able to come here for Christmas. It won't seem like Christmas to the children without their favourite uncle.

I've been busy decorating. The sitting-room walls are now a lovely butterscotch and all the woodwork is white. I'm tackling the kitchen at the moment. Terry is doing the tiling. You can imagine the chaos! He says it's not as easy as it looks!

Matthew phoned last night. He's enjoying the course at Plymouth, thank goodness, and seems to have made a lot of new friends.

e) With much love,

f) 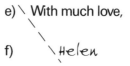Helen

g) P.S. We've acquired a tortoiseshell kitten which we're calling Benson. You'll love him.

Figure 2.3. The indented letter layout

b) The date

◆ Notice that the date starts in line with the beginning of the first line of the address.

◆ Always leave a space between the address and the date.

◆ There's always a comma in an indented layout date:
> Thursday, 21st October
> 21st October, 200-

◆ Use 21 October or 21st October, as you prefer.

◆ It's best not to abbreviate the day of the week, or the month. Write the words in full. Avoid 21/10/0-.

c) The salutation

◆ Note the comma after 'My dear Dermot'.

d) Paragraphing

◆ The indented layout is so called because each new paragraph begins 2–4 cm in from the left-hand margin. Some people like to start each new paragraph in line with the comma after the salutation; others indent a little to the left or right of this position. Certainly, it looks very attractive if each subsequent paragraph is indented by the same amount each time.

◆ There are no spaces left between paragraphs.

◆ Note that even though there is a comma at the end of the salutation, the paragraph that follows (like all subsequent paragraphs) begins with a capital letter.

e) The ending (or complimentary close)

◆ In an indented layout, the complimentary close is positioned in the right-hand half of the page. Some people like to place it in line with the address and date. This looks attractive.

◆ The first word of the complimentary close in both an indented and a fully blocked layout begins with a capital letter. Subsequent words are lower case:

Yours sincerely
With best wishes
Yours till the cows come home

♦ Note the comma at the end of the complimentary close in the indented layout.

f) The signature
♦ The signature begins slightly to the right of the complimentary close above. The slope of the address is repeated here.

♦ There is no need for a full stop after the signature.

g) Postscripts
♦ Note the position of the postscript. It is in line with the body of the letter.

INDENTED ENVELOPE LAYOUT

The address on the envelope should be indented too, to match the letter layout (see Figure 2.4).

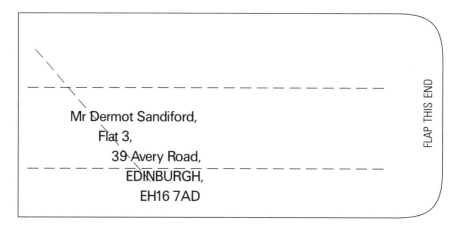

Figure 2.4. The indented envelope layout

♦ You will see that the name and the address are sloped or 'stepped'. Each line begins a little to the right of the line above.

◆ There is space at the top of the envelope for franking. If you start writing the name about half-way down the envelope, there is no danger that the franking will obliterate what you have written or typed.

◆ Note that each line is punctuated at the end, except for the postcode line. Replace the comma after 'Edinburgh' with a full stop if you prefer.

◆ The postal town and the postcode are capitalised, as in a fully blocked layout.

◆ A comma after the house number is optional.

◆ Leave space at the bottom of the envelope so that nothing is obscured when the enveloped is sorted en route.

Some Sample Letters Discussed

ABSENCE NOTE

Schools keep records of attendance and have to be able to account for all absences. It is, therefore, very important that parents and guardians write letters explaining the reason for their children's absence from school. Some schools file such letters.

See Figure 2.5 for a simple plan for such a letter.

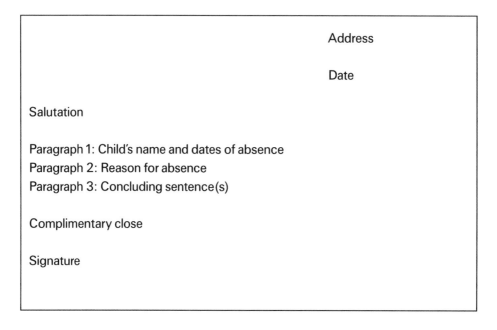

Figure 2.5. Plan for letter explaining absence from school

- ◆ Remember that it's preferable to use plain paper rather than lined.

- ◆ Take care to get the tone right. The letter should be courteous and friendly, as well as informative.

- ◆ Aim to write three paragraphs at least, if you can, even in a short letter like this one.

◆ This letter need not be posted. The child can take it to school on his or her return. It should, however, be sealed in an envelope addressed to the form teacher.

Here is an example of a letter written to the plan above.

Key Cottage
10 Long Causeway
BROCKHAMPTON
Cumbria
CA19 1TL

10 May 200-

Dear Mr Macmillen

Please excuse Sally's absence from school all last week.

She has been in bed with tonsillitis and a very high temperature. (She slept for the best part of three days!) Thankfully, she is feeling very much better now and Dr Grimes has confirmed that she is well enough to return to school.

I know that she will do her very best to catch up with the work she has missed.

Yours sincerely

Louise Carter
Louise Carter

Figure 2.6. Example of a letter explaining absence from school

Some useful spellings

appendicitis	flu (influenza)	penicillin
arthritis	gastritis	period pains
asthma	gastroenteritis	pneumonia
bronchitis	headache	psoriasis
Crohn's disease	measles	rheumatism
diabetes	medicine	stomach ache
diarrhoea	meningitis	temperature
earache	migraine	tonsillitis
eczema	orthodontist	vaccination
epilepsy	orthopaedic	whooping cough
erysipelas		

LETTER ASKING FOR A CHILD TO BE EXCUSED FROM GAMES

If the child has just returned to school after an absence, this request can be added to the absence note and the form teacher will pass on the request to the staff concerned.

The letter (Figure 2.7) is addressed directly to the games teacher because the child has not been absent.

Owl's Retreat
Rose Lane
PRIESTFIELD
EH16 1LY

18 October 200-

Dear Miss Peattie

I should be grateful if you would excuse Jane from games this afternoon.

She started a heavy cold over the weekend and she is still feeling rather feverish. She is subject to chest infections, as you know, and I want to take all reasonable precautions, short of keeping her home from school altogether.

I know you will understand.

Yours sincerely

Alison Comer

Alison Comer

Figure 2.7. Letter requesting excusal from games

LETTER EXPLAINING INCOMPLETE HOMEWORK

If there is a good reason why homework assignments have not been completed, parents can make life at school a lot easier for their children if they write a letter of explanation to each subject teacher concerned (see Figure 2.8).

◆ This letter, in a sealed envelope addressed to the subject teacher concerned, can be handed to the teacher by the child at the beginning of the next lesson.

---

110 Horsforth Road
FENCHURCH
Cleveland
TS10 9EW

12 November, 200-

Dear Mrs Lubbock,

Robert has not done the geography homework set for yesterday evening and I hope you will excuse this when you know the reason.

Robert got home from school yesterday just after 6 p.m., after the soccer match, with four homework assignments. By 11 p.m. he had completed only three: maths, history and French. He had worked conscientiously all evening, I can vouch for this, and he was just about to start your homework when I intervened. He looked exhausted and I made him pack up his books and go to bed. I promised him that I would write to you and explain.

Robert is anxious to do the work set. Would it be possible to allow him to do it over the weekend and hand it in next Monday? We would both be very grateful if you could agree to this.

Yours sincerely,

Tom Foy

Figure 2.8. Letter apologising for homework not done

◆ Notice that a clear explanation is given why the homework has not been done. Tom Foy is not blaming the school for overloading his son with homework. The tone remains courteous.

◆ Mr Foy makes it clear that his son doesn't want to evade the homework set by asking politely if a time extension might be possible.

Some useful spellings

anxious	difficult	language
assignment	embarrassed	literature
Business Studies	exhausted	mathematics
conscientious	frightened	tired
Design Technology	Information Technology	vocabulary

REQUEST FOR LEAVE OF ABSENCE

Parents and guardians have a statutory obligation to ensure that their children attend school if they are in good health. It can be a delicate matter asking for permission to take a child out of school for non-essential reasons. Schools discourage parents from booking family holidays in term-time, for example, even though they are aware that bargains are available outside the main school holidays.

Bear all this in mind when you ask for leave of absence. Make sure you have very good reasons for asking and make them clear courteously and firmly.

Give as much notice as you can so that the head teacher can consult your child's form teacher and subject teachers before replying.

The letter should be addressed to the head teacher and not to the form teacher (see Figure 2.9).

◆ It is clear that the parents will abide by the head teacher's decision without resentment.

◆ They do not take it for granted that permission will be granted but will be suitably grateful if it is.

◆ Note they have approached the school immediately they heard about the prize and realised the implications of the date offered. Let us hope the children will be allowed to go!

10 Roach Avenue
BARLOW
Gwynedd
LL29 4AE

4 May 200-

Dear Dr Stebbings

We have just heard that my husband has won first prize in a national electrical retailers' competition organised by Dansag. You can imagine how excited we all are by this. Part of the award is a three-week tour for all the family (all expenses paid) of China, Japan and the Philippines. Unfortunately, we have no choice over the dates. The holiday must be taken 1–22 July, and no adjustment is possible.

We realise that if Jack and Hannah come with us, as the prize envisages, they will miss the last three weeks of term. We know that the school discourages parents from taking children on family holidays in term-time, and we would not normally plan to do this. However, this unexpected prize is such a wonderful opportunity for the twins to see countries they would not otherwise have the chance to visit that we wonder if you might make an exception in this case. We have to confirm our acceptance of the prize holiday by 14 May. We will do nothing until we hear from you but we are hoping very much that you will give your permission for the children to accompany us on this holiday of a lifetime.

Yours sincerely

Michelle Staunton

Michelle Staunton

Figure 2.9. Letter requesting leave of absence from school

Some useful spellings

absence	grateful	sincerely
appreciate	guarantee	suppose
extremely	opportunity	surprise
family	realise	unfortunately

LETTER REPORTING BULLYING

If parents discover that their child is being bullied at school, it is important to inform the Head Teacher immediately. The school will have means of dealing with this as a matter of urgency.

♦ Parents may choose to telephone or visit the school at the first opportunity. It can, however, be helpful to outline the situation in a letter first (see Figure 2.10).

♦ The situation is a very painful one for both the victim and the parents of the victim, and the sample letter does not underestimate this.

♦ A firm but courteous tone is maintained.

♦ Action is expected.

Some useful spellings

behaviour	harass	regrettable
comment	insult	regularly
criticise (-ize)	intimidate	repetition
criticism	menace	situation
despair	possessions	systematic
desperate	regret	systematically

LETTER OF CONGRATULATION

Figure 2.11 is an example of a happy letter, sharing pleasure at hearing another's good news.

♦ This is a letter that can be written from the heart. Speak directly and simply to the recipient, and express your genuine delight.

♦ A letter of congratulation can all too easily sound gushing. Mention particular points of congratulation to keep it 'grounded'.

Telephone: (02392) 876543

123 Lensfield Road
Copnor
POTBURY
Hants
PO4 6SY

6 March 200-

Dear Mrs Gittings

Louise Scollen Form 8Y

I regret to say that Louise came home from school today in a very distressed state. It appears that she is being systematically bullied by three girls in her year.

It took me some time to get the full story from her. The bullying has been going on ever since she joined the school in January. She is a shy and gentle girl, and does not make friends easily. I suppose she has been an obvious target for callous bullies.

Books are taken from her desk, items of PE kit go missing, and hurtful remarks are made in the playground. They wait for her at the school gates and follow her home in a menacing way. Even worse, they have started to send text messages and phone calls so that she is not even safe from them in her own home.

She is asleep how, having sobbed her heart out and begging us to go back to Disbury where she was happy and had friends. She is so upset that I am not going to send her to school for the rest of this week. I know that it would be best to confront the bullies and put on a brave face, but she is not in a state to do this.

Louise knows that I am writing to you to explain the situation, and I think this is a relief to her. She has kept her misery to herself for too long and has despaired of there ever being an end to it.

You will know what steps to take. You will have encountered situations like this before. I just feel so angry that I want to tackle these girls myself, but this might make matters worse for Louise.

I shall deliver this letter by hand to the school in the morning and give you time to decide what should be done before I phone in the afternoon. We are all very upset.

Yours sincerely

Patricia Scollen

Patricia Scollen

Figure 2.10. Letter reporting bullying

The White House,
Musson,
NEWTOWNARDS,
Co. Down
BT92 3AZ

28 August, 200-

My dear Kieran,

I was so delighted to receive your letter and to learn that your place at Royal Holloway has been confirmed. It's a splendid college and I know that the history department there is particularly strong. I can see why RHUL was your first choice, and I am so pleased for you.

You thoroughly deserve your success. You worked hard for your excellent results and I'm so proud of you. It can't have been easy when you were dogged by glandular fever in Year 12 but you kept going when it would have been very easy to have given up altogether.

Well done, Kieran! I am tempted to give you lots of good advice that will keep you on the straight and narrow at university but you'll be glad to learn that I'm resisting the temptation!

I send you my best wishes for a very happy stay at university, studying the subject you've always loved.

Yours affectionately,
Elaine

P.S. You will allow a proud godmother to make a contribution towards your future expenses! I enclose a congratulatory postal order with all my love.

Figure 2.11. A 'good news' letter

Some useful spellings

absolutely	eventually	prestigious
achievement	finally	probably
always	granddaughter	receive
ambitious	manager	research
appointment	nephew	secretary
assistance	niece	success
career	opportunity	surprise
chief	parents	technical
college	pleasant	thoroughly
conscientious	possible	usually
decided		

LETTER OF CONDOLENCE

This is one of the hardest letters of all to write. However, even the briefest letter of sympathy brings great comfort to those who are grieving.

A possible plan would be as shown in Figure 2.12. A sample letter is shown in Figure 2.13.

Paragraph 1: Say how sad you are at the news.

Paragraph 2: Say what the person who has died meant to you.

Paragraph 3: Express your sympathy.

       (Avoid saying that you know exactly how they must be feeling, because you don't.)

Figure 2.12. Condolence letter plan

---

29 Priory Street
Redmore
BIRMINGHAM
West Midlands
BB2 6NJ

18 December 200-

Dear Mrs Doggett

I was so sorry to hear the sad news that Mr Doggett had died.

I worked for your husband in the 1990s and I shall always remember his kindness to me when I joined Chapplet and Gibson straight from school. It was a very happy office under your husband's management. Mr Doggett had the gift of being able to bring out the best in the people who worked for him. I know how very privileged I was to begin my working life there.

Your husband will be sadly missed by all who knew him. Please accept my deepest sympathy.

Yours sincerely

Elaine Peck

Elaine Peck

Figure 2.13. Sample condolence letter

LETTER OF APOLOGY

It is never easy to admit that we are in the wrong. Nevertheless there are situations where we have behaved badly, or made a false accusation or damaged property and so on, when an apology is called for.

◆ An apology should be wholehearted. It should:
  – admit the fault
  – express genuine regret
  – offer to make amends.

Katherine's letter to Jessica after an unfortunate accident is shown in Figure 2.14.

Some useful spellings

accept (please accept)	circumstances	moment
accidental	damaged	necessary
alcohol	decided	occurred
annoyed	definitely	restaurant
apology (plural -ies)	disastrous	sincere
appalling	embarrass	sincerely
behaviour	emergency	temperament
broken	extenuating	
casualty	irritate	

LETTER OF THANKS

We encourage our children to write thank-you letters for gifts received at birthdays and Christmases, and rightly so. We should respond gratefully to those who are generous to us.

As adults we will write thank-you letters on many other occasions too: in return for hospitality, for kindnesses, and other gestures of helpfulness and support (see Figure 2.15).

Saturday, 20 March

Dear Jessica,

I am so sorry. A dreadful thing happened last night. We were watching television and Dominic had just poured me a glass of red wine. I reached for it without looking properly and knocked the glass out of his hand and the wine went all over your beautiful carpet.

We were both horrified.

I'd heard that white wine is supposed to remove red wine stains and we tried this. It has helped a bit but the stain is still there as you'll see when you get back. We decided not to use any detergent on it in case we made it worse.

I've just phoned Chem-Clean (I found their number in the directory – 01932 867516) and they were quite optimistic about their being able to get the stain out once it is dry. I gave them the rough measurements of the carpet and they estimated it would cost £175–£200 to clean.

We have to leave today, as you know, and in any case I didn't like to make any firm arrangements to have the carpet cleaned without your permission. I'm enclosing a cheque for £200 made out to you. That will leave you free to choose the cleaning company you like best. If it costs more in the event, we insist on paying the balance.

If the stain doesn't come out, then we'll pay for a replacement carpet. That's the least we can do. You've been so kind to let us use your flat for a whole month. We've had a wonderful time – until this happened!

I'll ring you when you get back. I do hope we can sort this out (and that you have had a wonderful holiday).

With love and abject apologies,

Katherine

Figure 2.14. A letter of apology

---

147 The Crossways
PORTCHESTER
Devon
EX8 2EX

9 September 200-

Dear Mr Norman

I've got the job! They've just telephoned to offer it to me and I accepted immediately. From next Monday, I shall be the new administrative assistant at Rengolds! It's just the opening I've been looking for.

I'm so grateful to you for acting as my referee. I know how busy you are and it was so good of you to let me give your name in support of my application. I know it must have made all the difference.

Thank you once again. I can still hardly believe it.

Yours gratefully
Adam Little
Adam Little

Figure 2.15. A thank-you letter

◆ Note that 'thank-you' in a 'thank-you' letter is hyphenated. 'Thank' and 'you' are together forming a compound adjective and make one word.

◆ 'Thank you' in the last sentence of the letter is not hyphenated. It is short for 'I thank you'.

◆ Note too that just as it is courteous to ask permission to use a referee's name on an application form, so it is courteous to thank him or her afterwards (whatever the outcome).

Some useful spellings

appreciate	gorgeous	receive
believe	grateful	support
exciting	lovely	surprise
generous	present	useful

Part Two

◆ Business letters
◆ Job applications

3

Business Letters

Business letters are more formal than personal letters in a number of ways. After all, business letters are very often addressed to total strangers, in influential positions, about matters of some importance.

- Clearly your tone will be businesslike, while remaining respectful and courteous.

- The subject matter of your letter will be structured logically to make your point effectively. There will be no postscripts.

- You will take care to express yourself simply and clearly, avoiding the temptation to use pompous and long-winded words and phrases.

Don't be surprised if you need to make several drafts of an important letter before you are satisfied.

BUSINESS LETTER LAYOUTS

Business letters, like personal letters, can be either fully blocked or indented. Either layout is perfectly acceptable, although most firms have now adopted the fully blocked layout and will use this when writing to you. Use whichever layout you are most comfortable with and get it right every time.

The inside address

In a business letter, it is usual to include what is called the 'inside' address. This is the address of the person to whom you are writing, preceded either by his or her name, his or her job title, or both name *and* job title. To include an inside address is a sensible safeguard, as your letter may be opened by a secretary, and the envelope jettisoned, before it reaches the addressee. Moreover, in a large firm with other branches, your letter may be circulated in order to resolve a complaint or query and later be filed.

The usual position of the inside address is above the salutation, aligned against the left-hand margin in both indented and fully blocked layouts. Note, however, the inclusion of punctuation in the indented layout and its absence in the fully blocked one.

---

                                                9 Barnes Road
                                                TORVILLE
                                                Devon
                                                TQ6 1EY

                                                14 July 200-

The Managing Director
Permaglaze Ltd
Arda Industrial Estate
ROYNTON
Berkshire
PH3 3DF

Dear Sir or Madam

Figure 3.1. Fully blocked addresses

---

                                                9 Barnes Road,
                                                TORVILLE,
                                                Devon,
                                                TQ6 1EY

                                                14 July, 200-

The Managing Director,
Permaglaze Ltd.,
Arda Industrial Estate,
ROYNTON,
Berkshire,
PH3 3DF

Dear Sir or Madam,

Note: An alternative placing for the inside address is at the foot of the letter after the complimentary close and signature. It is still aligned to the left-hand margin in both layouts. There are examples of this alternative placing on pages 54 and 61. This positioning at the end of the letter is less common but it has the advantage of saving space at the beginning.

Figure 3.2. Indented addresses

The subject heading

It is helpful to the busy recipient of a business letter if the writer uses a subject heading. It identifies immediately the subject under discussion.

Notice the position of the subject heading in the examples that follow. The heading is placed below the salutation and above the beginning of the first paragraph. It is usually underlined.

In a fully blocked layout, the subject heading is aligned to the left (as you would by now expect). In an indented letter, it is centred.

Dear Sir

Changes to train timetables

I have been seriously inconvenienced by...

Figure 3.3. A fully blocked subject heading

Dear Sir,

Changes to train timetables
I have been seriously inconvenienced by...

Figure 3.4. An indented subject heading

The salutation (greeting) and the complimentary close

If the name of the recipient is used in the inside address above the salutation, then you will generally choose to use it in the salutation as well. The appropriate complimentary close will then be: Yours sincerely.

If the title and not the name of the recipient is used in the inside address, then the salutation will be appropriately formal:

Dear Sir
Dear Madam
Dear Sir or Madam.

Notice that 'sir' and 'madam' begin with a capital letter when used in a salutation.

Traditionally, the complimentary close to use with an impersonal salutation has been 'Yours faithfully'. You may, however, feel that even formal letters sometimes require a more cordial ending. Use 'Yours sincerely' in these cases. Use your own discretion but rest assured that 'Yours faithfully' is never wrong in a 'Dear Sir' letter and that in some cases it is the only appropriate ending.

Your signature

If your signature is not clearly legible, then print or type your name beneath it.

If you are a woman, it is courteous when signing letters to strangers to indicate how they should address you when they reply. Women who feel titles of address should have no connection with their marital status can use 'Ms' instead of 'Miss' or 'Mrs'. It is rarely necessary for men to put 'Mr' after their names but they should do so if their first name does not give a clear indication of gender. This is particularly true of 'foreign' names. Thus:

Esam Al-Sharae (Mr)

Note that the title or address follows the signature. Never sign yourself: Mr Esam Al-Sharae, Miss Alison Bennett, Mrs L. Brown.

If you have printed your name beneath your signature, then the title of address will follow this instead:

Yours faithfully

Esam Al-Sharae

ESAM AL-SHARAE (Mr)

THE ENVELOPE

Layout

The details on the envelope will repeat the inside address in the letter and will be fully blocked or indented to match the letter style. A reminder of the layout of a fully blocked envelope is shown in Figure 3.5.

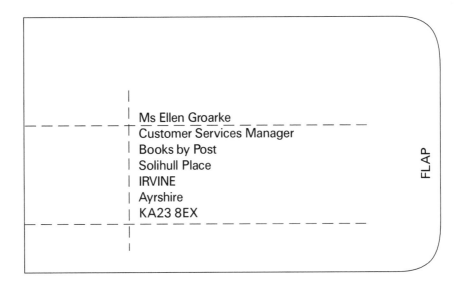

Ms Ellen Groarke
Customer Services Manager
Books by Post
Solihull Place
IRVINE
Ayrshire
KA23 8EX

FLAP

Figure 3.5. The fully blocked business envelope layout

Size

Consider using an A4 or A5 size envelope. If you have written your letter on A4 paper, you will avoid having to fold it if you use an A4 envelope and will have to fold it once only if you use an A5 one.

If your letter is an important one, it will look more businesslike if it emerges smoothly from the envelope. Don't spoil the appearance of a carefully written letter by folding it several times to fit into a tiny envelope. It won't lie flat ever again.

Some Sample Business Letters Discussed

LETTER REQUESTING INFORMATION

7 Mount View Avenue,
SOUTHAMPTON,
Hants,
SD18 4GY

30 April, 200-

The Customer Services Manager,
Beautiful Bathrooms Ltd.,
STOKE-ON-TRENT.

Dear Sir or Madam,

I was interested by your advertisement in today's 'Daily News' and I should very much like a copy of your current bathrooms brochure and price list.

I should also be grateful for a list of stockists.

Yours faithfully,
Jim Smith
Jim Smith

Figure 3.6. A letter requesting information

♦ This letter is appropriately brief and to the point. The writer just wants a brochure, a price list and information about stockists. That is all the Customer Services Manager needs to know.

♦ In a routine letter like this, the inside address can be shortened. The address on the envelope is:

The Customer Services Manager,
Beautiful Bathrooms Ltd.,
UNITS 8–15,
Wormley Industrial Estate,
STOKE-ON-TRENT,
Staffordshire,
ST2 9NZ

◆ 'Yours sincerely' could be substituted for 'Yours faithfully' in this straightforward request, even though the salutation is 'Dear Sir or Madam'.

Some useful spellings

accommodation	deposit	necessary
advertisement	discussed	prospectus
advice (noun: your advice)	enquiry	recent
advise (verb: please advise me)	enrol	receipt
appreciate	enrolled	receive
arrangements	enrolling	reception
believe	expect	recommend
brochure	expensive	representative
cancel	experience	requirement
cancelled	forward	reservation
cancelling	grateful	restaurant
cancellation	information	secretary
catalogue	intention	special
clerk	interested	subscription
confirmation	luxury	vegetarian
correspondence	manager	

LETTER EXPRESSING DISPLEASURE

There are bound to be situations from time to time that justify a letter of complaint: faulty goods, perhaps, or poor service, or lack of consideration.

Some such letters may be written more in sorrow than in anger; others may analyse the situation with icy clarity. The tone will be dependent on your relationship with the recipient. In all cases, however, it is important to wait until your initial anger has cooled before you write. You need to be sufficiently controlled to explain why you feel so strongly, to convince the recipient of your letter that there is a case to answer, and to make clear what action, if any, you expect by way of redress.

If you are writing to a company, ensure that you are writing your letter to the appropriate person. Phone the firm concerned to establish the name and the exact job title of the person who can best deal with your complaint. And aim high. Write to the man or woman in charge.

In the example letter (Figure 3.7), the writer is responding to unjustifiable criticism. She is replying to a letter and so knows both the name and job title of the misguided critic. She chooses, however, to keep the salutation and the complimentary close coldly formal.

- Note the tone of this letter: it is controlled, reasoned and dignified. The lofty reproof in paragraph four is calculated to find its target.

- The formal 'Dear Sir' and 'Yours faithfully' are exactly right here.

- An apology from Mr Wareham may or may not be forthcoming. It would, of course, be appreciated in a situation like this. However, the satisfaction in rebutting unfair charges coolly and incisively can be sufficient in itself.

Some useful spellings

apology	courier	expect
appalled	criticism	expensive
attention	customer	explanation
behaviour	damage	extremely
business	disappoint	faulty
broken	disaster	finally
collapse	disastrous	guarantee
complain	dismayed	impossible
complaint	dissatisfied	inadequate
complete	embarrass	inconsiderate ▶

8 Alwyns Close
EXMOUTH
Devon
EX8 2DP

11 February 200-

D J Wareham
Lettings Manager
Gibbons and Co. Estate Agents
64 High Street
EXMOUTH
Devon EX8 9BD

Dear Sir

I am writing in response to your letter of 9 February 200- objecting to the presence of builder's rubble in our garden.

I should first say that the tone of your letter is extremely regrettable. I take great offence at the insinuation that we are irresponsible members of Alwyns Close. We have lived here for almost four years and have good relations with virtually all the neighbours who own the maisonettes in the Close as well as with the tenants of the properties you manage.

The rubble in our garden is what is left of the bathroom which we have had refurbished. (I'd be particularly interested to know which species of vermin is attracted to plaster.) Much to our dismay, it has been there for just over two weeks, and so your statement that it has been there for 'some time' is rather exaggerated. We have had problems getting the builder to collect the rubble but after several phone calls we have finally managed to get his promise that it will be collected this Saturday (14 February).

In the circumstances either a phone call from you or a letter asking if there was a problem might have been more appropriate. I am very disappointed that you did not have the courtesy to take either of these options. I should also say that it is disappointing that the neighbour who complained was not able to mention their concern to us directly. Perhaps you might make this point to them.

We have spent a significant amount of money in improving this property and will shortly be putting it on the market. We had intended selling the property through Gibbons and Co. However, in the light of your letter, this is no longer the case.

Yours faithfully

Anna Sendall

ANNA SENDALL (Mrs)

Figure 3.7. A letter expressing displeasure

inconvenient	payment	replacement
initially	possible	reputation
irresponsible	present	restitution
manufacturer	quality	surprise
original	receipt	unacceptable
paid	receive	unsatisfactory

LETTER TO THE EDITOR

Letters to the editor may not always be printed in their full layout in the newspaper or magazine, but they should be presented to the editor as formal business letters, including the inside address. (See Figure 3.8.)

◆ Titles of newspapers need care. Check the masthead of the paper you read to see whether 'The' is part of the name. For instance, it is *The Times, The Sunday Times, The Mirror, The Sun, The Daily Express.* But it is: *Daily Mail, News of the World, Sunday Mirror, Sunday Express.*

```
                                                    Merrist House
                                                    29 Longdown Road
                                                    NEWTOWNARDS
                                                    Co. Down
                                                    BT29 8AX


                                                    11 November 200-


The Editor
The Belfast Bugle
110–112 Achill Road
BELFAST
BT15 3BU

Dear Sir

I read with interest Brian Kelly's comments on labels in Wednesday's issue (Letters:
10 November).

I also loathe labels, but not only the labels sewn into the necklines of shirts and
sweaters. I am driven mad by the labels that appear on fruit in shops and
supermarkets, horrid sticky little labels that are nowadays seen to be clamped to
every single apple, pear, kiwi fruit, orange and lemon.

I try to take them off when I am washing the fruit but they are a pest. They stick to
each other and they stick to me, and I get cross every time I try to get free of them.

I've found out that these labels are called PIPPLES. Pipples give me the pip! How do
other readers feel?

Yours faithfully
Lucy Pumphrey
Lucy Pumphrey
```

Figure 3.8. A letter to an editor

4

Job Applications

Look carefully at the seven advertisements in Figure 4.1. Answer the questions below by writing the reference letter(s) of the relevant advertisement(s) alongside.

i) Which advertisement specifies that the letter accompanying the curriculum vitae should be handwritten?

    _____

ii) Which advertisement requires the names, addresses and telephone numbers of two referees to be included in the application?

    _____

iii) Which advertisement would necessitate an initial letter requesting an application form?

    _____

iv) Which four advertisements specify that a curriculum vitae (a CV) should be submitted?

    _____ _____

    _____ _____

v) Which advertisement offers the opportunity to find out more about the post by clicking on to a website?

    _____

vi) Which three advertisements do not insist on relevant specialist qualifications?

    _____ _____

    _____

PLAYGROUP ASSISTANT REQUIRED

For

Happytots Playgroup

Preference will be given to applicants who have
a childcare qualification.

Applications should be sent to:

**Secretary, Happytots Playgroup,
The Community Centre, Cosham,
Portsmouth, Hants, PO2 9EL.**

The closing date is **Friday, 26th November.**

bostover | county council

(i) Maintenance Fitter
(ii) Maintenance Electrician

Are you looking for a challenging new career in Local Government offering:

- Job satisfaction;
- Excellent working conditions;
- Generous annual leave;
- Pleasant working environment.

Bostover County Council is inviting applications from suitably qualified persons who wish to be considered for inclusion on the following panels:

(i) Maintenance Fitter

(ii) Maintenance Electrician

If you are interested in these positions, application forms and full details are available on request from: J Conliffe, County Secretary, Bostover County Council, CASTLETOWN, Bostover, CA15 9QE

Completed application forms should be returned no later than:
4.00 p.m. on Thursday, 18th November.

Bostover County Council is an equal opportunities employer.

ARDMORE SQUASH CLUB
require:

SENIOR BAR PERSON

Reply in writing with C.V.
To: The Manager
Ardmore Squash Club
Breaffy Road, East Leake
Loughborough
LE1 2PE

OFFICE MANAGER/MANAGERESS

To take charge of busy office in our
Centra Shop/Filling Station.
Excellent Opportunities.
Please send CV to:
MARTIN KEARNEY
Centra Quick Shop/Texaco
Main Street, Grimsby DN8 2FF

Figure 4.1. Sample job advertisements ▶

(E)

ST. GERALD'S COLLEGE, CASTLEFORD
(Under the Trusteeship of the De La Salle Brothers)

Applications are invited for the position of

Administrative Assistant

Initially part-time with a view to becoming full-time.

Applicants should have excellent keyboard skills and excellent communication skills. Experience of working with young people will be an advantage. Handwritten letter of application and Curriculum Vitae to be submitted not later than 5.00 p.m. Monday, 8th November to:

Secretary, Board of Management,
St. Gerald's College,
Newport Road,
Castleford, NP2 7QS

(F)

LYMONE CASTLE
This wonderful 5-star luxury resort hotel is inviting applications for a

LEISURE CENTRE ATTENDANT

with benefits including:
ACCOMMODATION, UNIFORMS, & SICK PAY SCHEME
A Gym Instructor's Qualification is necessary, along with previous experience working in a similar environment.
Contact: **YVONNE O'DONOVAN** in Human Resources
Lymone Castle, BRIGHTON, BN2 5DL
Tel: 01273 687531 Fax: 01273 687543
Email: lymone@lymone.ie
Website: www.lymone.ie

(G)

HEADMASTER'S PERSONAL ASSISTANT/SECRETARY

Applications are invited for the above post vacant from September.
The person appointed will be experienced in the use of word processing, database operation and shorthand.
Normal office hours. Salary NJC 5 (based on 40 weeks/year)
Letters of application with CV and names, addresses and telephone numbers of two referees to:
The Headmaster, St Nicholas School, Melbourne Road, YORK, YO10 3QS by Monday 7 June.
Enquiries: 01904 561456

096699

Figure 4.1. Sample job advertisements (continued)

This section will offer advice on:

- preparing a curriculum vitae (a CV)
- requesting an application form
- completing an application form
- writing a covering letter to accompany a CV or application form
- writing a letter 'on spec' to a firm you would like to work for, asking about vacancies
- confirming attendance at interview
- accepting the offer of a post
- writing a resignation letter.

PREPARING A CURRICULUM VITAE (CV)

Increasingly, firms are mentioning CVs in their job advertisements or making it possible for you to send one by listing the kind of information about you that they wish to know. Some firms still issue, however, their own application forms which replace the CV.

A curriculum vitae is a brief but detailed account of your career up to the present time. When you compose your CV, you are really devising your own application form, enabling you to give the information that will show you in the best possible light.

To make a good impression on a prospective employer, a CV should be immaculately presented, with the information carefully spaced. It should look immediately attractive and be easy to read. Ideally, it should occupy no more than two sheets of good A4 paper. It should be accompanied by a covering letter. Covering letters are dealt with later in this section.

Ensure that your application looks pristine when it arrives at its destination by not folding the sheets to fit a small envelope. Invest in card-backed A4 envelopes.

Headings on a CV are used in the following order:

Name	Education
Address	Qualifications
Telephone number	Experience
Mobile number (if you have one)	Hobbies and interests (optional)
E-mail address (if you have one)	Referees (optional)
Date of birth (optional)	

There may well be other relevant headings you want to include. Insert them at suitable points.

Notice that all the headings are written in full. To abbreviate them would look too slapdash for this formal kind of document. Be warned also that ADDRESS, EDUCATION, QUALIFICATIONS, EXPERIENCE, INTERESTS, and REFEREES all present problems for uncertain spellers. Do check your spelling carefully, and get someone else to check your final version too. There is a list of useful job-related spellings at the end of this section.

Figure 4.2 is a specimen CV which we will look at in detail.

Name

Deborah has given her full name. She has chosen to indicate her marital status but she is not obliged to do so at this stage of the application.

Address

The full address including the postcode is given. Omitting an important detail could result in a delay in receiving an offer of an interview.

Telephone number

Deborah has chosen to give just her home number and mobile number. Give your work number here as well if you are permitted to receive personal calls and if your job application is not confidential.

CURRICULUM VITAE

NAME:	Deborah Alison Griffiths (Miss)
ADDRESS:	9 Barton Crescent, GREENTON, Northamptonshire, NN2 7HW
TELEPHONE:	(01536) 316043 (home)
MOBILE:	07752894164
DATE OF BIRTH:	9 August 1978

EDUCATION:

(1983 – 1990)	Greenton Church Primary School, Bicton Place, Greenton, NN11 8EX
(1990 – 1995)	Gerbraid Comprehensive School, Gipsy Lane, Greenton, NN11 3DF
(1995 – 1996)	Pilton Further Education College, Hele Road, Pilton, NN7 8BX

QUALIFICATIONS:

GCSE	English	B	1995
	English Literature	B	1995
	Mathematics	C	1995
	French	C	1995
	History	C	1995
	Geography	D	1995
RSA (Stage 1)	Keyboard Skills	Distinction	1996
	Bookkeeping	Distinction	1996
	Shorthand	Credit	1996

EXPERIENCE:

1998 – present day	Linton Tool Company Ltd., Broadfields Estate, Pilton, Northamptonshire, NN7 4FG

I am employed as an administrative assistant. My duties include typing, filing, processing time sheets, maintaining computerised sales records, and dealing with telephone enquiries.

Figure. 4.2. A specimen CV ▶

1996 – 1998	Granton Sales (Retail) Ltd., Rolle Street, Greenton, Northamptonshire, NN11 5BJ
	I had worked in Granton's as a sales assistant on Saturdays when I was at college. From time to time I had been entrusted with some of the ordering and the bookkeeping which I very much enjoyed. When I left college, I was offered a permanent full-time post as a junior clerk.

HOBBIES AND INTERESTS:

14 – 30s   This is a music and drama society which stages one major production a year. I have had a leading part in the last three productions.

Hockey   I play for Greenton Ladies' B team and I am also a member of the club's management committee.

Rowing   I am a keen member of Greenton and District Rowing Club.

REFERENCES   Mr. John Steward (Human Resources Manager)
Linton Tool Company Ltd., Unit 16,
Broadfields Estate, Pilton, Northamptonshire, NN7 4FG
Telephone: (01538) 919172

Dr. James Edgar (Principal)
Gerbraid Comprehensive School,
Gipsy Lane, Greenton, Northamptonshire, NN11 3DF
Telephone: (01536) 774866

Figure 4.2. A specimen CV (continued)

Date of birth

Deborah is young and she has given her date of birth. It serves to explain her brief career history. Nobody is obliged to include a date of birth on a CV. Omit it if you are a mature applicant and if you feel that your age might deter a prospective employer from calling you for interview. Remember that your CV and letter of application are designed to get you to an interview. At that stage, you will have the chance to convince the prospective employer that you are the best candidate irrespective of age.

Education

Deborah lists her primary and secondary schools to 'fill out' her CV. This is quite acceptable for a young candidate. More mature applicants, anxious to limit their CV to two A4 pages, may list just secondary school and college, or just college or university. Once again, there is no need to give dates of attendance.

Qualifications

Deborah has listed hers to look as impressive as possible. Notice how they are presented in order of merit. This is excellent. The busy prospective employer will glance quickly at them in the first instance, noticing the best results first.

Applicants with diplomas, degrees and professional qualifications will use the space to highlight these. They may summarise GCSE and A level results: 9 GCSEs (A – C); 4 A levels (A, A, A, B) or omit them altogether.

Don't include any examination failures or disappointingly low marks.

Use additional subheadings: RESULTS AWAITED (listing subjects and levels) and EXAMINATIONS TO BE TAKEN (listing subjects, levels, and the date when you plan to take them) if appropriate.

Experience

Your experience of the world of work should be listed in reverse chronological order, that is, with your current (or most recent) job first.

Deborah has mentioned her Saturday job at Granton's because it is to her credit that she was subsequently offered a permanent post there.

A candidate with a fuller work history would list only permanent posts.

Dates can be omitted, although length of service should be suggested.

Hobbies and interests

This is an optional entry. In Deborah's case, her interests help to supplement the other information on her CV and show her to be outgoing, sociable, active and responsible.

More mature candidates may not have the space to expand on hobbies and interests, but should do so if they are relevant to the post, of course.

Whatever happens, don't lie about interests or experience. If you go to interview, you might well be questioned about them by an enthusiast!

Referees

Deborah correctly gives her referees' full names, job titles, full addresses, and telephone numbers. (References are frequently sought over the telephone.)

Some applicants will not include referees' details on a CV but will be prepared to provide them when asked.

Choose your referees with great care. They should be people of some standing in the community (unrelated to you!) whose judgement can be trusted, for example: employer, head teacher, doctor or priest. The references they give will be in confidence and you should be sure they will speak well of you.

Always ask your referees' permission to quote their names. It is a courtesy to keep them informed on each occasion when their names are used, even if they have given you 'general' permission. It will give the opportunity too to tell them about the job you are applying for and what appeals to you about it. It will help them focus what they have to say about you and tailor it to the post.

A prospective employer may consult referees before shortlisting candidates for interview, or he or she may wait until making the final choice for the post. Whatever course is taken, the confidential assessment of your ability and character is going to be very influential. Remember too to let your referees know the outcome of your application. Thank them each time for their support whether you get the job or not.

Presentation

Keep the master copy of your CV in a safe place and make photocopies of it when needed. Remember to update it as time goes by. It is preferable to have your CV typed. A beautifully typed CV looks far more impressive than a handwritten one. Type on one side of the paper only.

LETTER REQUESTING AN APPLICATION FORM

A sample letter is shown in Figure 4.3.

COMPLETING AN APPLICATION FORM

These are the golden rules for form filling:

Take your time

Read the form carefully from beginning to end at least once, noting any special instructions:

◆ You might be asked to use block capitals throughout or in certain places.

◆ You might have to answer every question or write n/a against those that don't apply (n/a = not applicable).

Make a photocopy of the blank form

If the form is an important one (and a job application form always is), it is well worth making a photocopy of it to practise on.

```
                                        10 Mount View Avenue
                                        CASTLETOWN
                                        Bostover
                                        CA15 2NB


                                        15 November 200-


Dear Sir or Madam*

Vacancy for a Maintenance Electrician

I read with interest your advertisement for a Maintenance Electrician in today's
'Bostover Herald'.

I hold an HNC in Electrical and Electronic Engineering and I have ten years'
experience in the field.

I should very much appreciate further details of the post and an application
form.

Yours faithfully
Geoffrey Dwyer
Geoffrey Dwyer



J. Conliffe
County Secretary
Bostover County Council
CASTLETOWN
Bostover CA15 9Q3
```

*It would be efficient and courteous to telephone Bostover County Council and establish whether J. Conliffe is a man or a woman. Then you can greet the County Secretary appropriately in your letter.

Figure 4.3. A letter requesting an application form

◆ You then become familiar with the scope of the questions and avoid repeating information unnecessarily. You may see that there is provision for some details in answer to a later question.

◆ You can make sure that your answers fit comfortably in the space provided if you have practised on a photocopy first.

◆ There is often a question at the end providing half a page for you to explain why you think you are a suitably qualified candidate or why the post interests you. You will probably want to draft and redraft in rough your response to this. Your answer needs to be carefully structured and to be very well expressed. Once again, you will want your answer to fit the space provided comfortably. If you use a continuation sheet, make sure you have at least a respectable paragraph to add. A few words would look ridiculous.

Proofread your rough draft carefully

You cannot afford to ruin your chances by making a bad first impression. Spelling and punctuation should be perfect. Answers should give the information required. Your writing and expression should be clear. Ask someone else to check it for you if you have any doubts.

Complete the application form neatly

Once you are satisfied that your rough draft is as good as you can make it, complete the original.

◆ Be as neat as you possibly can.

◆ Use block capitals where required.

◆ Use black ink. It photocopies well, and photocopies may be made when it reaches its destination, one to each member of the interviewing panel.

Check it once again

Read it through carefully and ask someone else to check it too. Make any alterations as neatly and unobtrusively as possible.

Select a suitable envelope

If the form reached you in an A4 envelope, then use an A4 envelope to return it. If an A5 envelope was used (half the size of an A4 one), then use an A5 envelope. You want to avoid folding the form more than it has already been folded. Try to imagine how it will look when your prospective employer takes it out of the envelope.

Very important
Make a photocopy of the completed form before you post it.

- **This will be useful for future reference when you apply for other posts. Build up a file.**
- **It is always useful before the interview to be able to read again what you have written.**

You now need to write a careful covering letter.

WRITING A COVERING LETTER

Whether you are applying for a post by submitting your CV or by completing an application form, you will need to write a covering letter. The covering letter is sometimes called a letter of application, and that is exactly what it is.

In a covering letter, the information given in your CV or on the application form is not duplicated but everything relevant is discreetly highlighted. Establish what is 'relevant' by looking closely at the job advertisement, or by carefully studying information gained from the firm's website or from the job description that accompanied the application form (or all three).

Figure 4.4 is an example of a covering letter to accompany a curriculum vitae discussed earlier in this section. Deborah is applying for the post of Office Administrator.

- Deborah has telephoned Longwell Estates before writing this letter to find out whether the Human Resources Officer is male or female. 'Dear Madam' reflects the care she is taking with this application.

9 Barton Crescent
GREENTON
Northamptonshire
NN2 7HW

4 July 200-

The Human Resources Officer
Longwell Estates
FARNINGHEMBURY
Northamptonshire
NN21 8AA

Dear Madam

Vacancy for Office Administrator, Longwell Estates

I should very much like to be considered for the post of Office Administrator at Longwell Estates which was advertised in yesterday's edition of 'The Northants Messenger'.

I am currently employed as an administrative assistant at Linton Tool Company, Pilton. I enjoy my work there very much but there is little chance of promotion for some years and I should welcome the extra responsibilities offered by the post at Longwell Estates.

You will see from my curriculum vitae that among my GCSE passes I list the two subjects specified in your advertisement: English (B) and Mathematics (C).

There was no opportunity to take commercial subjects at school but I attended Pilton F.E. College and obtained RSA (Stage 1) Distinction in both Keyboard Skills and Bookkeeping, and a Credit in Shorthand.

I have discussed my application with my former Principal, Dr Edgar, and with the Human Resources Manager at Linton's, Mr. Steward. They have both urged me to apply for the post you have advertised and have kindly agreed to act as my referees.

I look forward very much to hearing from you and I do hope that I shall have the opportunity of an interview.

Yours faithfully
Deborah Griffiths
Deborah Griffiths

Figure 4.4. Example of a covering letter

- It is customary to state where you learnt of the vacancy. Deborah refers here to 'The Northants Messenger'. Newspaper titles should be enclosed within inverted commas or underlined.

- Deborah's application is strengthened by mention of her two referees having 'urged' her to apply. They clearly support her in her bid for promotion.

- She has made it quite clear that she is applying for the post of Office Administrator by using it as a subject heading. Always name the post. Firms may sometimes be advertising five or more posts at the same time, and your application may suffer from any confusion caused by your not being specific.

- It is usual to write rather than type a covering letter unless it seems particularly appropriate to type it. Use black ink rather than blue. Black ink photocopies better and your letter may be photocopied if you are to be interviewed by more than one person.

- Write on one side of the page only, and use plain paper, not lined. If you are nervous about writing on plain paper, use a sheet of heavily lined paper underneath as guidelines.

- Use A4 paper. It will be the same size as your CV or application form.

- Keep a photocopy of your letter. Indeed, keep everything relevant to each application you make: the job advertisement, CV, photocopy of the job application form, the covering letter, etc. You will find this invaluable if you are called to interview because you can check again all the information you have been given by the firm concerned and all the information you have given them. Such a file is also useful for future applications. You have models to work from.

- Make sure that your application looks fresh and attractive when it appears before your prospective employer. Use a card-backed A4 envelope. Avoid having to fold the pages.

- Ensure you use stamps to the right value by weighing your package before posting it. You don't want your prospective employer to have to pay excess postage and you want to ensure that it goes by first-class post. If you can, deliver it by hand to avoid any possible delay.

Note: Your aim at this stage is to be invited for interview. There may be 200 or more applicants. From these, a shortlist of five or six candidates will be made. You want to be one of those five or six. Once you have secured an interview, you will have the chance you need to prove that you are the most suitable candidate for that particular post.

WRITING A LETTER 'ON SPEC'

We have dealt so far in this section with applications for vacancies that have been advertised. It is well worth approaching other firms to ask if there might be a vacancy in the near future for which you would be eligible.

If the firm is expanding or if it is known that someone working there will be retiring, emigrating, or leaving for some other reason, your enquiry and availability could save the firm the onerous task of advertising and sifting responses. You may be just the person they are looking for.

Writing a letter 'on spec' like this is very much like writing the letter of application in response to an advertisement. It is only the introductory and closing paragraphs that will be different. (See Figure 4.5.) You will, of course, enclose a copy of your up-to-date CV.

Ensure you are addressing your letter to the appropriate person in the firm (name and job title) by phoning in advance and asking the receptionist.

The plan of your letter will be basically this:

◆ introductory paragraph giving your reasons for writing to the firm (perhaps relocating, looking for more responsibility, imminent redundancy)

◆ main body of letter outlining qualifications and experience and highlighting relevant features on your CV

◆ closing paragraph courteously offering to provide referees' names and addresses if these are not included in your CV and any other information that may be required.

31 Bembridge Road
GLOUCESTER
Gloucestershire
GL1 8EF

9 August 200-

Mr Robert Barnes
Workshop Controller
Arvon Coachworks
LITTLEHAM
Derbyshire
DE21 6SB

Dear Mr Barnes

I shall be moving to Derby in October. I wonder if there might be the possibility of a vacancy in your workshop for a qualified mechanic.

As you will see from my CV, which I enclose, I hold City and Guilds qualifications in Motor Vehicle and Light Vehicle Craft Studies and I have worked for thirty years in the motor industry. I am a qualified MOT tester and have had responsibility for developing new MOT business and for training and supervising staff in a small workshop.

I know of Arvon Coachworks by reputation and I should welcome the opportunity of joining the team should a possibility exist.

I am very happy to provide any further information that you may require, including the names and contact details of my referees.

Yours sincerely

Alan Seattle

Alan Seattle

Figure 4.5. Example of a speculative letter

◆ It is always tricky getting the right tone in such letters. Aim to be confident (but not arrogant) and courteous (but not grovelling). Write as many drafts as necessary until you get it right, and then keep a copy. This copy can provide the model for other such 'on spec' letters if you are unsuccessful in this enquiry. Keep a careful list also of firms you approach, with dates.

LETTER CONFIRMING ATTENDANCE AT AN INTERVIEW

This is always a courteous gesture. It enables the interviewing panel to schedule arrangements with confidence and it also shows how serious you are in your application.

---

42 Everton Drive
CAMBRIDGE
CB1 7DW

28 May 200-

Dear Mrs Parkinson

Thank you for your letter of 23 May inviting me to interview at the school on June 10.

I shall arrive at 11 a.m., as you suggest, for a tour of the school and accept with much pleasure your invitation to lunch with the governors before my interview at 2.30 p.m.

Yours sincerely
Charles Dobson
Charles Dobson

Mrs T.F. Parkinson
Secretary to the Governors
The King's School
PETHERBRIDGE
CB11 9EL

Figure 4.6. Letter confirming attendance at an interview

LETTER OF ACCEPTANCE

Always confirm in writing your acceptance of the offer of a post. (See Figure 4.7.)

42 Everton Drive
CAMBRIDGE
CB1 7DW

28 May 200-

Dear Mrs Parkinson

Thank you for your letter received today.

I am delighted to accept the governors' invitation to join the English Department as an NQT.*

I enjoyed my visit to The King's School on June 10 very much indeed and look forward to the beginning of term on 9 September.

Yours sincerely

Charles Dobson

Charles Dobson

Mrs T. F. Parkinson
Secretary to the Governors
The King's School
PETHERBRIDGE
CB11 9EL

*NQT is a newly qualified teacher

Figure 4.7. Letter accepting the offer of a post

LETTER OF RESIGNATION FROM PRESENT POST

In order to take up a new post offered by another firm, you will have to resign from your present post. 'Handing in your notice' is often done informally by word of mouth, but you will sometimes be asked to confirm it in writing (see Figure 4.8).

◆ Be tactful, however delighted you are to be leaving. Aim to be warm and appreciative, if you can, about your time with your present firm.

Ivy Cottage
3 The Green
LUSCOMBE
AL3 2RW

10 October 200-

Edward Hughes
Area Supervisor
Harp Dairies Ltd
Rougemont Industrial Estate
LUTON
LU23 7HA

Dear Mr Hughes

As requested earlier today, this is to confirm formally my resignation from my post with Harp Dairies.

I shall serve my month's notice, and make my last delivery on 12 November, as agreed.

My eight years working for Harp have been very happy ones. It is a very good firm to work for and I have always been treated fairly. I shall miss the rest of the team and the routine.

However, I look forward to additional responsibilities in my future position with Abbott Dairy Products. This is an opening that I cannot afford to refuse.

Thank you for all the help and support you have given me since I joined Harp.

Yours sincerely

John Regan

John Regan

Figure 4.8. Letter of resignation from present post

◆ Give a reason for leaving, if you possibly can. Here, 'additional responsibilities' is perfectly acceptable, and enables your present employer to wish you all the best in your new post.

◆ Remember you want to leave on good terms if you possibly can. One day you might want to come back (in a senior position, of course!). Don't burn your boats.

Some useful spellings

accurate	choice	enthusiasm
achieve	circumstances	enthusiastic
achievement	clerical	environment
address	clerk	especially
advertisement	colleague	examination
annual	college	excellent
anxious	committee	experience
application	complete	explain
appointment	confident	explanation
appraisal	conscientious	
appreciate	consultancy	faithfully
arrange	consultant	file
assistant	convenient	filing
association	currently	flexible
attach	curriculum vitae	formal
available		formally
	decide	fulfil
benefit	decision	fulfilled
benefited	different	fulfilling
build	discuss	further
bureau		
business	eager	government
	education	grateful
career	efficiency	guidance
careful	enquire	
challenging	enquiry	honest

incentive

increase

increment

information

initial

initially

initiative

intention

interest

interested

interview

language

leisure

liaise

liaison

maintain

maintenance

management

manager

managing

managing director

mathematics

mechanic

necessary

negotiate

opportunity

organise

particular

permanent

permission

pilot

pleasure

position

possibility

possible

practical

privilege

procedure

processing

professional

qualification

qualified

qualify

receive

referee

reference

relevant

representative

resign

resignation

resources

responsibility

responsible

safety

salary

schedule

secretary

separate

similar

sincerely

situation

society

solicitor

special

studied

succeed

success

suggest

technical

technician

technological

technology

temporary

theoretical

theory

training

useful

vacancy

variety

Part Three

◆ Formal invitations and replies

5

Formal Invitations and Replies

Most of the social invitations we receive are informal ones. A friend telephones to invite us for a meal; we accept or regretfully decline there and then. Friends or family write to invite us to stay for a few days; we respond informally in the same way ('John and I would love to come. Thank you very much. See you next Saturday.').

Formal invitations, however, are very different. They have their own conventions.

WEDDING INVITATIONS

The wedding invitation is the formal invitation with which the majority of us are most familiar.

Look closely at the three examples that follow (Figure 5.1) and note all the conventions they share.

- All three invitations are written in the third person. The reply, which we discuss later in this section, will similarly be couched in the third person (Mrs Betts has great pleasure in accepting...).

- They are all printed, not typed or handwritten.

- Space is left on all three for the name(s) of the invited guest(s) to be completed by hand. (This is never typed.)

- All three are similarly formulaic:
  – request the pleasure of the company of

- All three structure the invitation in the same way:
  – church, date, time, reception

(A)

Brigadier and Mrs Stephen Cecil
request the pleasure of the company of
. . . .
at the marriage
of their daughter
Edwina
to
Mr William Ferdinand Fitzgerald
at Holy Trinity Church, Bexley,
on Saturday, 5th June 200- at 2 o'clock
and afterwards at The Chandos House Hotel, Pilton

RSVP
Bellruth Cottage
Bexley
Sussex TN10 3HR

(B)

Martin and Isobel Harper
request the pleasure of the company of
. . . .
at the marriage of their daughter
Louise
to
Clive Declan Montescue
at The Church of the Nativity, Exford,
on Saturday, 12 June 200- at noon
and afterwards at
Figgins Gallery, Exford

RSVP
Figgins Gallery
Church End
Exford, Devon
EX2 9E2

(C)

Naomi Denver and Terence Harris
request the pleasure of the company of
. . . .
on the occasion of their marriage
at St Mary's Church, Loxton,
on Friday, 28th May, 200- at 1 p.m.
and afterwards at a reception in
The Longford Arms Hotel, Longford.

Boleyard   RSVP
Stambridge   1st May 200-
Derbyshire, DE5 3HS

Figure 5.1. Wedding invitations

◆ They all ask for a reply and supply an address. RSVP is a contraction of the French 'Répondez s'il vous plaît' which means 'Please reply'.

You may, however, have noticed some differences:

◆ In the first two invitations, it is the bride's parents who are issuing the invitation; in the third, it is the bride and groom themselves. This is a perfectly acceptable variation and may indeed be more appropriate if the couple have been living together before deciding to get married.

◆ There are gradations of formality here, with the first invitation being more formal than the second which is more formal than the third.
  – In the first invitation the titles of the bride's parents are used (Brigadier and Mrs Stephen Cecil). They are not used in invitation b) (Martin and Isobel Harper).
  – The name of the groom is given in full in the first two invitations (Mr William Ferdinand Fitzgerald; Clive Declan Montescue). In the third, we have the names of the couple simply given (Naomi Denver and Terence Harris).

The firm you entrust with the printing of your wedding stationery will have a variety of styles to show you. Take time to decide on the wording and the spacing. They matter even more than the font and the type of card.

OTHER FORMAL INVITATIONS

We will look at examples of another type of formal invitation before considering the formal reply of acceptance or refusal. You will see that they are very close to the wording and style of the wedding invitations.

The Board of the Linenhall Arts Centre invites

. . . .

to the official opening
of the newly developed Linenhall
by Dermot O'Shea
Minister for Arts, Tourism and Sport
on Thursday 25 November
at 4.30 p.m.

RSVP
The Linenhall Arts Centre
Londonderry
LD6 9FP

Mr and Mrs Tom Hughes request the pleasure of the company of

. . . .

at a Dinner-Dance to be held at Armitage Lodge, Cardiff
on Saturday 24 April at 8.15 p.m.

RSVP
17 Payhembury Close
Payhembury
CF8 19YF

The Directors of the Omega Foundation invite

. . . .

to a reception
at The Palace Hotel, Torquay
on Tuesday, 26 October 200-
at 1900 hours
to welcome the Cultural Delegation from the USA.

RSVP
The Omega Foundation
Stiford Manor
Newton Abbot
Devon , TQ5 9AJ

Figure 5.2. Three types of formal invitation

FORMAL ACCEPTANCE

The reply to each formal invitation should match its style in every way. These would be the replies to the three wedding invitations bearing in mind the slight gradation in formality.

Ⓐ

> 73 Knowsley Road
> Portchester
> Hants
> PO12 7FE
>
> Mr and Mrs Allardyce accept with great pleasure the kind invitation of Brigadier and Mrs Stephen Cecil to attend the wedding of Edwina and William at Holy Trinity Church, Bexley, on Saturday 5th June 200- at 2 o'clock and the reception afterwards at the Chandos House Hotel, Pilton.
>
> 14 May, 200-

Ⓑ

> 73 Knowsley Road
> Portchester
> Hants
> PO12 7FE
>
> John and Helen Allardyce accept with pleasure the kind invitation of Martin and Isobel Harper to attend the wedding of Louise and Clive at The Church of the Nativity, Exford, on Saturday 12 June 200- at noon and the reception afterwards at Figgins Gallery.
>
> 30 May, 200-

Ⓒ

> 73 Knowsley Road
> Portchester
> Hants
> PO12 7FE
>
> John and Helen Allardyce thank Naomi and Terence for the kind invitation to attend their wedding at St. Mary's Church, Loxton, on Friday 28 May, 200- at 1 p.m. They accept with great pleasure and look forward also to the reception afterwards at The Longford Arms Hotel, Longford.
>
> 15 April, 200-

Figure 5.3. Three types of formal acceptance

- Note that all replies are in the third person.

- If titles are used in the invitation, then they are in the reply. Mr and Mrs John Allardyce accept (invitation A); John and Helen Allardyce accept (the other two invitations).

- The details are repeated (church, date, time, venue for reception) so there will be no confusion.

- The address of the person replying is given, to avoid any confusion of identity.

- The date of writing, if given, appears in the bottom left-hand corner.

- Note that there is no salutation, no complimentary close and no signature.

- The reply may be either handwritten or typed on unlined paper.

- If the invitation came from both parents, the envelope will be addressed to the mother. In the case of the invitation from the bride and groom, address the letter either to the bride or to the pair of them.

FORMAL REFUSAL

The formal refusal, like the formal acceptance, will match the style of the invitation in every way. It is courteous to give a brief reason why you cannot accept.

The examples in Figure 5.4 would be acceptable replies expressing inability to attend the last three formal invitations.

- These formal refusals follow the same pattern as the formal acceptances in repeating the details of the invitation but there is no need to refer to the time of the function.

- These refusals can seem rather cold, albeit correct. It would not be wrong to enclose a personal note with the formal refusal, hoping the event is a great success and regretting your unavoidable absence. On the other hand, it is not necessary! It will depend on how well you know those issuing the invitation.

73 Knowsley Road
Portchester
Hants
PO12 7FE

John and Helen Allardyce thank the Board of the Linenhall Arts Centre for their kind invitation to attend the official opening of the newly developed Linenhall by Dermot O'Shea, the Minister for Arts, Tourism and Sport on Thursday 25 November. Unfortunately they will be in Mexico for the last week of November and will be unable to attend.

10 November 200-

73 Knowsley Road
Portchester
Hants
PO12 7FE

Mr and Mrs John Allardyce thank Mr and Mrs Tom Hughes for their kind invitation to attend a Dinner-Dance at Armitage Lodge, Cardiff on Saturday 24 April. They regret they will not be able to attend as they have a prior engagement on that date.

8 April 200-

73 Knowsley Road
Portchester
Hants
PO12 7FE

Mr and Mrs Allardyce thank the Directors of the Omega Foundation for their kind invitation to attend a reception at The Palace Hotel, Torquay on Tuesday 26 October to welcome the Cultural Delegation from the USA. Regretfully they will be unable to attend as Mr Allardyce is convalescing from a serious heart operation.

10 October 200-

Figure 5.4. Three types of formal refusal

Part Four

- ◆ Classified advertisements
- ◆ Family announcements

6

Classified Advertisements and Family Announcements

CLASSIFIED ADVERTISEMENTS

Advertisements in newspapers are divided into two main categories: classified and display.

Display advertisements are often illustrated and have elaborate layouts spread over a number of columns. Their cost is calculated according to the space they occupy. Classified advertisements, on the other hand, are small advertisements taking their place in single columns under relevant headings such as, 'Lost and Found', 'Articles for Sale', 'Accommodation to Let'. These advertisements (or small ads) have the same typeface and layout as each other and are charged according to the number of words used.

There are a number of occasions when you might want to place a classified advertisement in your local newspaper. If you study other advertisements in the classification that interests you, you will find that there is a kind of formula to the wording that will be a useful guide. Examples will be given here of insertions in some of the most popular categories.

You will see that you need to be concise but, at the same time, you will want to include everything that is relevant. Remember that the staff in the newspaper office concerned will help you with the wording if needed but it is best to list beforehand all the details you want included.

Try composing the advertisement yourself. Abbreviations can be used for economy's sake (they count as one word) but they must be widely recognised, like WLTM in the Encounters column and s/c in the Accommodation to Let. These abbreviations will be listed at the end of the section.

CLASSIFIED ADVERTISING

SMALL ADS GET RESULTS! Reach 59,718 homes!

Print your ad below in BLOCK CAPITALS, one word in each box

- 80p a word (min. 10 words)
- tel. nos. count as two words
- add £2.50 if box number required and count as one word.

No. of words:_____

Classification required:_____

Name:_____

Address:_____

Figure 6.1. A typical classified advertisement form

Articles for sale

Aim to say just enough to interest a potential buyer; you can go into more detail when the interested reader telephones you.

It is usual to give a contact telephone number. If you want to limit calls to after-work hours, then include this. (A telephone number usually counts as two words.)

Here are four sample advertisements. Note that the first word is usually printed in bold type, and your wording can take advantage of this by placing the keyword first.

Dining table and 6 chairs. Excellent condition. Suit rental property. £200 secures. (01396) 217902

Piano, upright, iron frame. £250. Can deliver. (01847) 928196

Washing machine, tumble dryer and dishwasher. Can be seen working. Owner emigrating. (02345) 987561 after 6 p.m.

Three-piece suite, two-seater sofa, two armchairs, cottage style, button back, heavy cotton upholstery. vgc. £125 ono. (07788) 675448

Articles wanted

This can be a useful 'last resort' if you have searched unsuccessfully for something through the usual channels.

1996 edition of Chambers 21st Century Dictionary. Must be in good condition. (03956) 214890

Good quality logs required for woodburning stove. Delivery essential. (09481) 269507

Accommodation to let

You will find a huge number of abbreviations used here. There will be a list (with definitions) at the end of the section.

Three examples follow. First a single room, then a house-share and lastly an unfurnished house are advertised.

Room to let with own bathroom. Cheltenham outskirts. N/S only. No pets. Refs required. £220 pcm inclusive. (01242) 377077 after 5 p.m.

Professional person required to share house with two others. City centre. En-suite dble. room. All mod. cons. £280 pcm. (08713) 698881

4 bed unfurnished house with garage. 3 rooms en-suite. Southampton central. Suit professionals or family. OFCH. £420 pcm. (01752) 985318

Accommodation wanted

Urgently required. 6 bed property for family relocating to Llandudno. To £1000 pcm. (01397) 829565

Lost and found

Lost – pet kitten. Colour ginger/white/black. Landford area. Info. gratefully received. (09876) 793815

Lost – in Portaleigh area Saturday evening, gold charm bracelet. Sentimental value. Reward offered. (08795) 205194

Found – Sat. 18 April. Black Labrador, white patch on neck. Lovely obedient dog. (08691) 843260

Found – Small teddy bear with one ear missing. Red scarf round neck. Exeter City Centre. Saturday. (01392) 987130 after 6 p.m.

Situations wanted

It is well worth placing an advertisement in 'Situations Wanted' when you are job-hunting. You may be just the person a potential employer is looking for and you'll save him or her the work of advertising and shortlisting.

Use a box number if you want to protect your anonymity. The newspaper concerned will allocate the number. Replies to your advertisement will be addressed to them and collected from them or forwarded to you.

Retired nurse available for home nursing in the Birmingham area. Apply in writing to Box No. 668.

Childminder available to mind children in her own home. Pollingford area. After-school service also available. Keen rates. (01784) 961496

Bookkeeper available for part-time employment. Experience in Debtors/Creditors ledger, PAYE and VAT returns, wages and general office duties. Computer experience in Office Accounts. Tel. 0878951003

Mature man. 45 yrs. Own retail business for ten years. Fit, good with people, clean driving licence, farming experience. Seeks new challenge. Please contact Steve on 071 306921

Lonely Hearts/Encounters/Social and Personal

This advertising classification has a rich list of abbreviations all its own. They will be included with other abbreviations at the end of the section. (Payment in this classification is often by the line.)

Quiet F 50, enjoys music, walking, films, theatre, crosswords, history, seeks M 42–60 GSOH sim. ints. Photo and phone number apprec. Cambridge area. Box 865

Attractive professional female 35. GSOH. Likes travel, gardening, classical music, seeks M 30–50 for f/ship. London. Box 947

Looking for love, tall slim M 28, grad., n/s, s/d, seeks fun-loving F for LTR. Box 912

M 68 WLTHF home-loving widow 50+ for f/ship. ALA Box 529

FAMILY ANNOUNCEMENTS

Local newspapers have columns detailing births and deaths. Quality national newspapers also have a section for these and for engagements and marriages.

Births

Here are six sample announcements.

COMER – on 20 October 200-, to Delia (née O'Brien) and Kevin, twin daughters, Abigail Denise and Jennifer Anne.

HUDSON – on 21 October 200-, at Exworthy Hospital, to Agnes and Stephen, Robert, a brother for Ceri and grandson for John and Helen, Harold and Edith.

LEWIS – Anna June was born at Kidderminster General Hospital on October 19, 200-, the first child of Henrietta and James.

MADVANI – on 20 October at Swansea District Hospital to Diviya (née Mehrota) and Nikesh, a son, Eshan.

POPE – on October 22, to proud parents Carol and Adrian, the precious gift of a daughter, Cressida Jane.

WILLIAMSON – Henry and Emma proudly announce the birth of Jack on 20 October at Houston Maternity Clinic. Thanks to all midwives and doctors, Uxbridge and Houston.

Engagements

Mr P. J. Hobbs
and Miss R. Stebbings
The engagement is announced between Peter, son of Mr and Mrs Alan Hobbs, of Belfast, Northern Ireland, and Rachel, only daughter of Dr and Mrs Guy Stebbings, of Darlington, Co. Durham.

Mr C. W. Littler
and Miss C.A. Legge
The engagement is announced between Charles, son of Mr Alan Littler of London and Mrs Susan James of Exeter, and Chaunia, daughter of Mr and Mrs Leo Legge, of Torquay, Devon.

◆ Notice the wording here. Charles Littler's parents are divorced and his mother has remarried.

Mr A. C. Davitt
and Mrs K. L. Yeomans
The engagement is announced between Andrew, son of Mr and Mrs Henry Davitt, of Stockport, and Kate, daughter of the late Mr Joseph Carson and of Mrs Carson, of Emsworth, Hants.

♦ Notice the wording here. Kate Yeoman's father has died but he is still mentioned. It is Kate's second marriage.

Marriages

Marriages, like engagements, continue to be announced formally in the quality national press, but are rarely announced in the local press. A local newspaper is more likely to print a wedding photograph if submitted with a caption. Here is an example of a formal announcement of a marriage.

Mr R. B. Potts
and Miss L. E. Elsevier
The marriage took place on 23 November, 200-, at St. Colman's Church, Cosham, Hants. between Mr Roger Potts and Miss Lynn Elsevier. Canon Gordon Snelworth officiated, assisted by Fr. Nicholas Jeffery.

The bride, who was given in marriage by her father, was attended by Miss Rachel Pegg, Miss Susan Kramf, Megan and Kayleigh Sendall, and Jeremy Brunton. Mr Matthew Moore was the best man.

A reception was held at the Devereux Arms, Southsea, Hants.

Deaths

Some newspapers will require verification of deaths before accepting an announcement, to avoid malicious and unfounded insertions. Even if the Funeral Director submits the final wording, you will need to be consulted.

Here are a few sample announcements as a guide.

HOLLIWELL – On May 7th, Charles Frederick, aged 81, of Goldsmith Road, Preston, beloved husband of Winifred, loving dad of Pat, Tom and

Jimmy, and darling granddad of Simon. Funeral service St Thomas Methodist Church, Friday May 14th, 11 a.m., followed by interment Exwick Cemetery. Flowers to M. Roche and Sons, 20 Holloway Crescent, Exwick, by 9.30 a.m.

GRANTHAM – On June 9th, at her daughter's home, Tower View, Aldtown, Alice Mary, beloved wife of the late Randolph and dear mother of Jock and Phyllis, a loved grandmother and great-grandmother. Funeral service at the Aldwych and Aldtown Crematorium on Wednesday 16 June at 12.30 p.m. Family flowers only, please.

OCKLEY – On August 8th, at Bodwell District Hospital, Sara, aged two weeks, darling daughter of Beth and Keith. Requiem Mass at St. Etheldreda's, Bodwell, on Thursday 12 August at 11.00 a.m. No flowers by request.

WENTWORTH – Peacefully at home, on 21st September, Anne, (née Phillips) of Peterborough, beloved wife of Walter and much loved mother of Pauline and Roger. A most wonderful person who will be missed by all who knew her. Private cremation. No flowers, please, but donations, if wished, to Arthritis Research c/o Pepper, Lavelle and Kilcoyne, 64 High Street, Bronsgrove, Worcs., B61 8EX.

Acknowledgements

GRANTHAM Alice Mary – Jock, Phyllis and families would like to thank all those who attended her funeral service and everyone who sent cards, letters and messages of sympathy.

In Memoriam

OCKLEY Sara (1st Anniversary) – In loving memory of our daughter, Sara, who died last year on 8 August. Always in our thoughts.

Some abbreviations used in classified advertisements

acv (ACV)   air-cushioned vehicle

air con	air conditioning (car)
ALA	all letters answered (Lonely Hearts)
ALAWP	all letters answered with photograph (Lonely Hearts)
a/new	as new
bed/bdrm	bedroom
bth	bath/bathroom
c/h (C/H)	central heating
c/o	care of
cv (CV)	curriculum vitae
dbl/dble	double
div.	divorced
DR	dining room
DSS	Department of Social Security
ea	each
esr	electric sunroof (car)
F	female
ff	factory-fitted (car)
f/f (FF)	fully fitted (kitchen), fully furnished
fsh (FSH)	full service history (car)
f/ship	friendship (Lonely Hearts)
GCH	gas central heating
gge	garage
grad	graduate
GSOH	good sense of humour (Lonely Hearts)
h + c	hot and cold (water)
ho	house
inc	inclusive
info	information
k + b	kitchen and bathroom
LTR	long-term relationship (Lonely Hearts)
M	male
M/F	male or female
mod cons	modern conveniences (accommodation)
n/d (N/D)	non-drinker
n/s (N/S)	non-smoker
OFCH	oil-fired central heating
ono	or near(est) offer
pcm	per calendar month
p/t (P/T)	part-time

pw	per week
refs	references
r/ship	relationship
s/c	self-contained (accommodation)
s/d (S/D)	social drinker
s/history	service history (car)
sim ints	similar interests (Lonely Hearts)
SOH	sense of humour
s/roof	sunroof (car)
t + s	toilet and shower
T + T	taxed and tested (car)
TT	teetotal(ler)
vg	very good
vgc	very good condition
VGSOH	very good sense of humour (Lonely Hearts)
whb	wash-hand basin
WLTM	would like to meet (Lonely Hearts)
WLTHF	would like to hear from (Lonely Hearts)

Part Five

- ◆ Notice of meeting and the agenda
- ◆ Minutes
- ◆ Posters and handbills
- ◆ Press releases

7

Committee Meetings

If you are at all involved in your local community, there may well be a time when you find yourself elected to a committee. (You may perhaps belong to a sports or social club, or be involved in local politics, or actively support your local school, church or favourite charity...)

The time may also come when you are asked to serve on that committee as Hon. Sec., the honorary (= unpaid) secretary. What will your duties be? Correspondence? Minutes? Publicity? Some committees expect the secretary to be responsible for all three areas; others may appoint a special Minutes Secretary to be responsible solely for the minutes, leaving the Hon. Sec. free for the rest. Some committees appoint one committee member to be solely responsible for publicity.

In this section, we will explore and exemplify the conventions of the range of written forms the Hon. Sec. may have to handle:

- notice of meetings
- agendas
- minutes
- posters and handbills
- press releases.

NOTICE OF MEETING AND THE AGENDA

It is usual for the Hon. Sec. to send a written notice of a forthcoming meeting to every committee member seven to ten days in advance, unless agreed otherwise. Such a notice is very brief. Indeed, the details have probably been agreed at the last meeting and so the notice may serve merely as a reminder.

The agenda is usually enclosed at the same time. The notice and the agenda can be on the one A4 page, signed by the Hon. Sec.

The format of the notice of meeting is usually a simple sentence:

> The next committee meeting will be held at (place) on (date) at (time).

The agenda is a list of topics to be discussed at the meeting. 'Agenda' is Latin for 'What must be done'. The Secretary and the Chairperson will draw it up together.

The first three items on an agenda and the last two are always the same:

> Apologies for absence
> Minutes of the last meeting
> Matters arising
> ....
> ....
> ....
> Any other business (AOB)
> Date of next meeting

The notice and agenda of the next committee meeting of St Sidwell's School PTA might look something like Figure 7.1.

MINUTES

The minutes of a meeting are a brief account of the business conducted there. They are a summary of the important points of discussion and a record of decisions reached.

Those entrusted with the responsibility for writing up the minutes of any meeting will make careful notes during the course of it. The exact wording of motions, the names of those proposing and seconding them, and the outcome of the votes should always be included in the minutes.

St Sidwell's School Parent-Teacher Association

Dear_____

The next committee meeting will be held at the school on Friday 21 May at 7.30 p.m.

Agenda

1. Apologies for absence

2. Minutes of the last meeting

3. Matters arising

4. Summer fête: Saturday 26 June

5. Chess Club: new organiser needed

6. AOB

7. Date of next meeting

Alan Hobbs

(Hon. Sec.)

Figure 7.1. Example of a notice of meeting and agenda

You will see from the example on pages 94 and 95 that minutes are written in the third person ('The Secretary was asked ...' Not 'I was asked...') and in the past tense, and follow the headings of the relevant agenda.

Minutes of the previous meeting are either read aloud to the committee by the Hon. Sec. when they next meet (to check that they are a fair and accurate record of what took place) or copies are distributed beforehand (with the notice of meeting and the agenda) for committee members to study in advance. Any corrections can be made before the minutes are signed by the Chairperson.

There are various ways of writing up minutes. Some record discussions in great detail; some simply list resolutions reached and the names of those responsible for carrying them out. Some strike a happy medium between these two extremes. Study the past minutes of your organisation to help you maintain a similar format and tone.

Minutes of St Sidwell's School PTA Committee held at the school on Friday 21 May, 200-.

Present: John Comer (Chair), Josephine Hall, Margaret Hughes, Charles LeMin, Noel McNicholas (Staff Representative), Carmel O'Brien, Stephen Sinclair, Brian Bell (Treasurer), Alan Hobbs (Secretary).

Apologies for absence: Michael Mullen, Pat Pumphrey.

Minutes of the last meeting: The minutes of the meeting held on 26 April were read and approved (proposed Brian Bell, seconded Carmel O'Brien).

Matters Arising: Noel McNicholas reported that the Healthy Food Tuck Shop was now up and running, and very popular with the pupils. The letter to parents requesting help with staffing the shop had resulted in twenty volunteers coming forward. A rota has been organised.

Summer Fête: Saturday 26 June
The Chairperson reminded the meeting that £1,800 had been raised the previous year. It was a real challenge to aim to better that. Some new ideas, as well as the old favourites, would be needed. Noel McNicholas confirmed that each class would organise the same stall as before: Lucky Dip, Toy Stall, Book Stall, Cake Stall, Fishing Game, and Spin-a-Plate.

After some discussion, it was agreed that committee members would be responsible for the following stalls and activities, and would recruit additional helpers:

Fortune-telling: John Comer
Plant stall: Charles LeMin
Garden produce: Stephen Sinclair
Guess the weight of the cake: Margaret Hughes
Tail on the Donkey: Alan Hobbs
Refreshments: Carmel O'Brien & Josephine Hall

It was hoped that Pat Pumphrey would once again do Face-Painting. The Secretary would contact her.

The possibility of hiring a Bouncy Castle was discussed. It was agreed it would need to be carefully supervised to check over-boisterous activities. Three adults would be needed at a time: one to collect shoes and breakable objects like spectacles, one to take the money, and one to supervise the 'bouncing'. The Secretary agreed to investigate the cost and report back at the next meeting.

Figure 7.2. Sample layout for minutes of a meeting ▶

Charles LeMin suggested that it might be worth contacting Paulsgrove Primary in the hope of borrowing their Wheel of Fortune. It was a real money-spinner. If Michael Mullen took over responsibility for the Plant Stall, he would be willing to organise the Wheel of Fortune. The Secretary agreed to contact Paulsgrove Primary, and he would explain the situation to Michael Mullen.

It was agreed unanimously (proposed Carmel O'Brien, seconded Stephen Sinclair) that a larger float, £20, was needed for each stall this year. It was also agreed that the Treasurer would remain based in the dining hall and stall holders would deliver takings to him during the afternoon at their convenience. Charles LeMin asked if a careful record could be kept of each stall's takings so stall-holders would know at the end how much each had raised. This was agreed.

Chess Club: The Secretary reported that a new parent-volunteer would be needed in September to run the Chess Club as the Carson family were moving to Scotland. As members knew, Michael Carson had started the Chess Club in 1992 and both the under-8 and the under-11 teams had done extremely well in the Inter-Schools League. It would be a great pity if the club had to close.

It was agreed unanimously (proposed Margaret Hughes, seconded Josephine Hall) that a letter should be sent to parents asking for a volunteer to take over.

The Secretary was asked by the Chairperson to write a warm letter of thanks to Michael Carson for all he had done for the school and wishing his family all the best in the future.

It was agreed unanimously (proposed Charles LeMin and seconded Alan Hobbs) that a presentation should be made to Michael on behalf of the PTA at the last meeting of the Chess Club in July.

AOB: Stephen Sinclair showed members a fund-raising tea towel brought home by his son from the Dolphin Kindergarten. Pupils' self-sketches and names had been printed in blue on a white ground with the name of the Kindergarten clearly displayed. He suggested that St Sidwell's might consider approaching the same company, and offered to investigate further. This was welcomed by those present.

Date of next meeting: Friday 4 June at 7.30 p.m.

The meeting closed at 9.25 p.m.

Figure 7.2. Sample layout for minutes of a meeting (continued)

Figure 7.2 illustrates a simple, fairly standard example of minutes made at a PTA committee meeting. Only the main points of the discussion are summarised and the decisions reached are clearly stated. They will serve as a very practical reminder of decisions made and will be useful for future reference.

♦ Note that the venue and date (but not the time) are carefully included in the heading.

♦ Those present are listed: Chairperson first, other officers last, and the rest in alphabetical order in between.

♦ Apologies for absence are also listed in alphabetical order. Names only are recorded and not the reasons for absence. The Secretary will have received some apologies in advance. Others will be passed via other committee members at the beginning of the meeting. Apologies do not have to be formally written ones; they can be telephoned or offered informally. It is, however, a courtesy not to be overlooked.

♦ Once the minutes have been approved, the Chairperson signs them. They are kept carefully for future reference as an undisputed record.

POSTERS AND HANDBILLS

The Committee of St Sidwell's PTA may want to attract the general public as well as parents and pupils to their summer fête. Parents can be informed by a photocopied letter sent home with their children. The general public can be targeted in a variety of ways: posters, handbills, car stickers, display advertisements and features in the local press, and announcements on local radio.

Do make sure that no vital information has been omitted. Look closely at the car sticker and the display advertisement for a local newspaper (Figures 7.3 and 7.4). What has been accidentally left out?

Car stickers and display advertisements are expensive publicity items. Such a pity to have omitted the venue in the first and the time in the second!

SAY **NO** TO THE
INCINERATOR

PUBLIC MEETING: SATURDAY 14 MARCH
8 p.m.

ALL WELCOME

Admission Free

Figure 7.3. Car sticker. Spot the omission.

ST SIDWELL'S PRIMARY SCHOOL

SUMMER FÊTE

SATURDAY 26 JUNE

Dozens of stalls & activities:
books, toys, cakes, garden produce

LUCKY DIP   BOUNCY CASTLE
FACE PAINTING
WHEEL OF FORTUNE

Refreshments & Ice creams

ALL WELCOME   Admission **20p**
                        at gate

Figure 7.4. Display advertisement. Spot the omission.

All publicity material should answer these five vital questions:

- ◆ What
  What is the event?
- ◆ When
  When will it take place (date and time)?
- ◆ Where
  Where will it be held?
- ◆ Who
  Who can come? Who is taking part?
- ◆ How much
  How much will it cost?

As Honorary Secretary of your association, you may find it helpful to keep examples of all publicity material you produce. It can be easily modified for future repeat occasions.

PRESS RELEASES

Some events for which your committee is responsible may be newsworthy, locally or nationally. Presenting a press release is a well-established way of approaching journalists with a possible news item.

A press release may be printed as it stands, or it may be followed up by a reporter and 'developed' into a much bigger feature. Either way, a press photographer may be sent to cover the event. Such publicity can be very welcome to an organisation.

Press releases aim to catch the attention of news editors as they glance casually at the opening paragraphs. Be brief, positive and informative. Remember the 5 W's: who, what, when, where, why. These are the details that the news editor will want to know.

A skilful press release is planned so that the most important information is at the beginning. It can be shortened, if newspaper space is limited, from the end upwards. Perhaps the last paragraph will be cut or the last two, or three.

Each paragraph may be very interesting as it examines the 5 W's in great detail, but detail is expendable if space is at a premium.

Always give a contact name and phone number at the end and the date, so that the story can be followed up.

If photographs are enclosed, ensure that a condensed version of the press release heading is pasted on the back, with the caption.

Figure 7.5 is an example of a press release, submitted to a local newspaper by the Parish Assistant of the Sacred Heart Church in Exebridge.

Explanatory notes

a) The heading is informative, and sums up the story. It doesn't have to be 'snappy'. You can leave that to the professionals.

b) The date is made very clear. 'Next Saturday' is too imprecise on its own.

c) By the end of paragraph two, the 5 W's have been covered: what, when, who, where, why.

d) In a local newspaper, details such as addresses and schools attended will be of interest. This is not necessarily true of the national press.

e) Try to include some direct quotations. They enliven the account.

f) Write 'ends' at the end of the press release. If more then one page is used, write m/f in the right-hand corner of preceding pages. (m/f = more follows). Number the pages.

g) Always provide a contact name and title. The title indicates how the contact is involved in the event. Daytime and evening telephone numbers and a mobile number (if available) should also be given here.

h) The date given is the date the press release is composed, not the date of the event described.

Finally, press releases should be double spaced, with wide margins, and typed or written on one side of the paper only. This helps the editor and the typesetter. There is plenty of space for additional material and instructions to be added in the newspaper office.

a)   SPONSORED HYMNATHON at SACRED HEART CHURCH, EXEBRIDGE

b)   On Saturday next (12 October), 14 members of the choir of the Sacred Heart Church in Exebridge will begin the longest choir practice of their lives. They will start at 9 a.m. and they don't intend to stop until 9 p.m. that evening, twelve hours later.

c)   But this is no ordinary choir practice. It is a sponsored hymnathon. Their choir-mistress, Lydia Carter, of Lodestone Road, explains: 'We want to raise as much money as we can between us. The bell-tower is in a dangerous condition and we'd like to help pay for its restoration in time for the church's centenary celebrations next March.'

d)   The youngest choir member taking part is Elena Morgan, 14 years, who is in Year 9 at Exebridge Comprehensive. Elena has raised the promise of £268 of sponsorship money if she can keep going until the 9 p.m. deadline. The eldest is Jim Atkins, 83 years, of Seymour Avenue. 'I may

e)   not be able to keep going to the end,' he said, 'but I'll do my best. Every hour of my sponsor money will mean another £30 for the bell-tower.'

Every member of the choir will be allowed two half-hour breaks whenever it best suits them. The rest of the choir will carry on singing. They will be accompanied by a rota of three organists: Pam Sedgewick, Bill Greenwell, and Nancy Wells. 'We plan to work our way through the parish hymnal,' says Pam. 'We'll play the ones we know, and then we'll start again.'

m/f

Figure 7.5 Example of a press release ▶

Parishioners are enthusiastic in their support. 'I think they're marvellous,' said Rose Cussell, who lives nearby in Raddenstile Lane. 'I'll be in the church with them for as long as I can manage. They deserve our support.'

Fr. Larry Costello, Parish Priest at the Sacred Heart, is full of admiration for his choir and he plans to sing alongside them.

Anyone willing to sponsor the event should contact Fr. Costello, (01951) 761476. And if you can drop in at the church, any time between 9 a.m. and 9 p.m. next Saturday, you'll be very welcome indeed.

Choir members taking part are: Jim Atkins, Cheryl Bending, Claire Benzies, Sam Carter, Debbie Lake, Alan Lumsden, Elena Morgan, Roger Norris, Jean Roberts, Di Sturgess, John Tucker, Priscilla Tucker, Becky Wills, and Jacob Williamson.

f)   (ends)

g)   Jane Byrne
      (Parish Assistant)
      (01951) 831297 (day)
      (01784) 223984 (evenings)
      07357903487 (mobile)

h)   6 October 200-

Figure 7.5. Example of a press release (continued)

Some useful spellings

absence

advertise

advertisement

agree

agreed

aloud (= out loud)

allowed

  (= permitted)

amend

amendment

annual

apologise (-ize)

apology

appoint

approve

arrange

business

circulate

circumstances

committee

confidential

constitution

convenience

convenient

correspondence

criticise (-ize)

criticism

decide

decided

decision

disagree

disappoint

disapprove

discussion

distribute

eligible

exercise

expenses

expensive

experience

grateful

likely

motion

necessary

occasion

occasionally

opinion

opportunity

passed (the motion was

  passed)

past (in past years)

period

permanent

persuade

possibility

possible

presentation

prevent

proposal

propose

prove

quorum

receive

regular

regularly

release

relevant

representative

resign

resignation

responsibility

responsible

secretary

sincerely

situation

subscribe

subscription

success

successful

suggest

suggestion

support

surprise

temporary

treasurer

unanimously

venue

volunteer

Part Six

◆ Punctuation

8

Punctuation

CAPITAL LETTERS

Capital letters should be used to begin:

* sentences
* proper nouns
* main words in titles
* direct speech
* references to the Deity and sacred books
* lines of poetry
* the salutation and the complimentary close of a letter.

In addition a capital letter is always used:

* for the pronoun 'I'.

Sentences

Use a capital letter at the beginning of each sentence, whether a statement, a command, or a question:

* This house is not for sale. (statement)
* Is your house on the market? (question)
* Sell your house and bank the money! (command)

Proper nouns

Proper nouns are specific names for people, places, etc. and not to be confused with common nouns which are general names, not requiring an initial capital:

girl (common noun)   Sinead (proper noun)

city (common noun)   Exeter (proper noun)

day (common noun)   Wednesday (proper noun)

Proper nouns include:

◆ forenames and surnames	Anna Browne
◆ titles	Dr Grimes, Mrs Hughes, Sir Matthew Eveleigh
◆ countries, nationalities, languages	Italy, Spanish, Urdu
◆ towns, cities, counties	Westport, New York, Hampshire
◆ streets	Acacia Avenue, Roehampton Road
◆ names of houses	Key Cottage, Sandiford House
◆ days, months, festivals	Monday, September, Christmas, Diwali
◆ historical periods	the Middle Ages, the Industrial Revolution
◆ geographical features	Mount Everest, the River Thames
◆ companies and organisations	The Sunlight Laundry, Dr Barnardo's Homes
◆ political parties	The Freedom Party

Note:

a) Seasons of the year do not need initial capitals when they stand alone but they do when attached:

We shall see her next winter.
We are going to the Winter Olympics.

b) School subjects don't need initial capital letters but languages do:

Ben is studying geography and Russian at evening class.

Main words in titles

Use a capital letter at the beginning of the first and last words in a title and at the beginning of every keyword in between:

Gone with the Wind
The Adventures of Huckleberry Finn
The Diary of a Provincial Lady
The Daily Telegraph
News of the World

Direct speech

When quoting the actual words spoken, always begin with a capital letter, even if the quotation comes mid-sentence:

She looked at me sternly before saying, "Well, I take people as I find them."

References to the Deity and sacred books

God, Yahweh, Allah
the Bible, the Koran, the Vedas

Note: Pagan gods have initial capitals: Neptune, Zeus, Ceres, but they are referred to as 'gods' not 'Gods'.

Lines of poetry

Conventionally, each line of poetry begins with a capital letter (but some modern poets dispense with this).

Since there's no help, come let us kiss and part –
Nay, I have done, you get no more of me;
And I am glad, yea, glad with all my heart,
That thus so cleanly I myself can free.

Michael Drayton

Letters

The salutation begins with a capital letter:

> Dear Mrs Atley
> Dear Adrian
> My dearest love

The complimentary close always begins with a capital letter:

> Yours sincerely
> With best wishes
> Until next week

The pronoun 'I'

Always use a capital letter for 'I' even when it forms part of a contraction:

> You know I would never let you down.
> You know I'd never let you down.

FULL STOPS

Full stops (.) are used:

- ◆ to mark the end of a statement
- ◆ to show that a word has been shortened.

To mark the end of a statement

The difficulty here is recognising when a statement has ended. A very common error is to string statements together with commas when they should be separated by full stops:

> ✗ The meeting was adjourned at 12 noon, only five people had bothered to turn up, the organisers agreed that insufficient notice had been given.

✓ The meeting was adjourned at 12 noon. Only five people had bothered to turn up. The organisers agreed that insufficient notice had been given.

How does one recognise a statement? Does it help to say that a statement is complete in itself and it can stand alone? Read the three statements again in the example above and pause after each of them. Can you feel the 'completeness' of each of them?

Separate statements like this can be combined into a single statement by rewriting and by adding conjunctions (joining words like: if, although, when, as, because, so that, and, but, or...). There are so many different ways that probably few people would combine them in the same way. This is where personal style comes in. You may want to reword your own sentences several times until you feel you have the best possible order with the right emphasis.

An example: As only five people had bothered to turn up, the organisers adjourned the meeting at 12 noon, agreeing that insufficient notice had been given.

See also 'semicolons' and how they can be used in an example like this to join sentences.

To show that a word has been shortened

You will be familiar with many of these:

B.B.C.	(British Broadcasting Corporation)
P.T.O.	(Please turn over)
R.S.V.P.	(Répondez s'il vous plaît – Please reply)
Mr. Brown	(Mister Brown)
G. K. Chesterton	(Gilbert Keith Chesterton)

You will probably also be aware that modern typing and printing practice is rapidly banishing this use of the full stop:

BBC, PTO, RSVP, Mr Brown, G K Chesterton

The use of full stops to mark abbreviations is largely discretionary now. Use them if you wish; omit them if you wish, but be consistent.

Note: if the last word in your sentence ends with a full stop indicating an abbreviation, you will not need another one to show the statement has ended. The single full stop will do double duty:

✗ The film ends at 11 p.m..
✓ The film ends at 11 p.m.

QUESTION MARKS

Question marks (?) indicate the end of direct questions (= the actual words used by the person asking the question):

Will you marry me?
Why are you crying?
What is the time?

If, however, the question is reported to another person, it becomes a statement. A full stop is then the appropriate end stop:

He asked me if I would marry him.
My mother asked me why I was crying.
I asked them the time.

EXCLAMATION MARKS

Exclamation marks (!) are used with:

◆ commands shouted at the top of one's voice
◆ expressions of really strong feeling
◆ exclamatory phrases and sentences.

Shouted commands

The exclamation mark registers on paper the volume of the voice shouting the command:

"Be quiet, all of you!" shouted the exasperated teacher.

Note, however, that if the command is reported later to someone else, it becomes a statement, and a full stop is the appropriate end stop:

He told us all to be quiet.

Expressions of strong feeling

May you rot in hell!	(curse)
God bless you!	(blessing)
Thank you so much!	(gratitude)
Help!	(panic)
Hear! Hear!	(heartfelt agreement)
Ugh!	(disgust)
Hooray!	(joy)
Wow!	(amazement)

Note that if such a brief expression is part of a longer sentence, there are two ways of punctuating it:

Good heavens! You gave me a fright.
Good heavens, you gave me a fright!

Exclamatory phrases and sentences

Use an exclamation mark at the end of exclamatory phrases and sentences beginning with:

What a...!
What...!
How...!

What a wonderful person!
What energy you have!
How ridiculous!

Other exclamatory sentences might begin with:

If only...!
To think...! and so on.

If only I'd known you were coming, I'd have met you at the airport!
To think that you came to England without telling me!
I can't believe you said that!

COMMAS

Commas are used to mark a pause in a sentence. There are many situations where a pause is needed to clarify the meaning.

Lists

◆ Commas are used to mark off each item in a list so that the reader's eye can make sense of the structure of the sentence immediately. Commas restore order, as you can see here:

✗ I bought three loaves tomatoes garlic two pounds of onions a chicken and three lettuces.

✓ I bought three loaves, tomatoes, garlic, two pounds of onions, a chicken and three lettuces.

Use a comma before the final 'and' if you wish. Sometimes you have to use a comma with 'and' to avoid confusion. There is no possible confusion in the example above, but read these examples:

? For this recipe, you need chicken, garlic, dried tomatoes and onions. (Do the onions have to be dried too?)

✓ For this recipe, you need chicken, garlic, dried tomatoes, and onions. (Answer: No, they don't!)

Note: Sometimes the confusion may be only momentary. The reader gets half-way through a sentence, realises it makes no sense, and has to start again. A comma can save this confusion:

> The café was empty and full of litter. (empty and full?)
> The café was empty, and full of litter.
> I reversed the car and the dog started barking. (reversed the car and the dog?)
> I reversed the car, and the dog started barking.

If you always use a comma before the final 'and' in a list, you'll always be on the safe side. It is never wrong to use a comma with 'and'; it is sometimes essential.

Terms of address

Names, endearments and other terms of address are separated from the rest of the sentence with a comma or a pair of commas. A pair of commas will be needed if the term of address is used mid-sentence:

> Madam, your taxi has arrived.
> Your taxi has arrived, madam.
> Your taxi, madam, has arrived.

Interpolations

Interpolations are words and phrases like:

> well
> however
> please
> of course
> in fact
> oh

Commas are used to separate these from the main structure of the sentence. Once again, a pair of commas will be needed if the interpolation occurs mid-sentence:

Well, it's really entirely up to you.

Oh, don't take him so seriously.

You will, of course, be very welcome.

Please, let me come with you.

We've decided to move to Scotland, as a matter of fact.

Apposition

Commas are used to mark off words and phrases in apposition. Look at these two sentences:

My youngest son, James, loves sailing.

James, my youngest son, loves sailing.

Both sentences mean the same thing, although the word order is different. 'James' and 'my youngest son' are one and the same person. Whichever term comes second in the sentence is said to be in apposition to the first, and is separated by a pair of commas.

If you were saying the sentence aloud, you would pause a little and offer the word or phrase in apposition as an extra piece of information. The pair of commas is a way of indicating this on paper:

On August 9th, my birthday, we're going out to dinner.

My cousin, Audrey O'Leary, is retiring this year.

His prize, a dictionary, was specially inscribed.

Pauses

Use a comma to indicate a pause. Long sentences often need to be read with a pause here and there. A comma will make sure that the reader pauses in a sensible place:

Miss Wills put aside her sewing and hobbled into her tiny kitchen to start preparing her supper, although she was not really very hungry.

Non-defining clauses

Don't be alarmed at this technical term. It is just a useful form of shorthand.

See what a difference to the meaning commas make here:

> The pupils who wanted extra homework waited by the teacher's desk at the end of the lesson. (i.e. those who didn't want extra homework left the room)

> The pupils, who wanted extra homework, waited by the teacher's desk at the end of the lesson. (i.e. every pupil wanted extra homework)

Read the two sentences aloud, pausing at each comma in the second sentence. Spoken aloud, the difference in meaning is clear. On paper, commas are needed when the clause is non-defining (i.e. applies to *all* described):

> The firemen, who wore protective clothing, were unhurt. (= all the firemen wore protective clothing)
> The firemen who wore protective clothing were unhurt. (= only those wearing protective clothing were unhurt – the rest...)

> The five secretaries, who have diplomas in word-processing, are to be given a pay rise. (= there are five secretaries. All of them will get a pay rise. They all have diplomas in word-processing.)
> The five secretaries who have diplomas in word-processing are to be given a pay rise. (= only five secretaries will get a pay rise – the ones with word-processing diplomas.)

Direct speech

Note the use of commas in the following three sentences of direct speech. (There will be a fuller discussion of direct speech when we come to inverted commas.)

> She said, "I am sorry to disturb you."
> "I am sorry to disturb you," she said.
> "I am sorry," she said, "to disturb you."

Participial phrases

Once again, a technical term has had to be used which will sound alarming if it is unfamiliar. There is no need to be alarmed.

Look at the following examples of participles introducing phrases, and notice how they are separated from the rest of the sentence by a comma or a pair of commas. The participles are underlined:

Glancing at her coldly, he walked past. (present participle)
She watched him, fuming inwardly, but said nothing. (present participle)
The car, polished lovingly, looked almost new. (past participle)
Terrified by their threats, the youngster cowered against the wall. (past participle)

Note: Be very careful with the placing of a pair of commas in a construction like this:

✓ He rang the doorbell nervously and, attempting to look confident, put his hands in his pockets.
✗ He rang the doorbell nervously, and attempting to look confident, put his hands in his pockets.

Participial phrases are rather like the interpolations and the phrases in apposition we have already discussed. They add extra information and can always be omitted without the structure of the sentence being affected. If you leave out the participial phrase in the correctly punctuated example above, the sentence reads:

He rang the doorbell nervously and put his hands in his pockets.

The word 'and' must not be enclosed with 'attempting to look confident'. The main sentence needs it.

APOSTROPHES

Apostrophes (') are used for two separate reasons:

- to indicate possession   (John's moustache)
- to indicate missing letters   (I'm very sorry.)

Possessive apostrophes

The possessive apostrophe is used to indicate ownership:

my father's briefcase	(the briefcase of my father)
my friend's cottage	(the cottage of my friend)
the boys' shirts	(the shirts of the boys)
the women's umbrellas	(the umbrellas of the women)

There is a very straightforward way of knowing where to place the apostrophe. (You don't need to worry about singular and plural nouns and whether the plural is formed by adding -s.) Use this four-step method and you will never make a mistake:

Step 1: Identify the owner.
Step 2: Put an apostrophe immediately after this word.
Step 3: Add -s if the word doesn't already end in -s.
Step 4: Name the possession.

Here are some examples of how the steps work. See how apostrophes help you to write more concisely:

- the voice of the teacher

1) Who is the owner of the voice?	= the teacher
2) Put an apostrophe immediately after.	= the teacher'
3) Add -s if there isn't one already.	= the teacher's
4) Name the possession.	= the teacher's voice

- the voices of the teachers

1) Who are the owners?	= the teachers
2) Put the apostrophe immediately after.	= the teachers'
3) Add -s if there isn't one. (There is.)	
4) Name the possession.	= the teachers' voices

♦ the toys of the children

1) Who are the owners?	= the children
2) Put the apostrophe immediately after.	= the children'
3) Add -s if there isn't one.	= the children's
4) Name the possession	= the children's toys

Note: With proper nouns ending in -s (e.g. Charles Dickens, John Keats), you have the choice of adding an -s if you wish when indicating ownership (Step 3):

✓ Charles Dickens' novels
✓ Charles Dickens's novels
✓ John Keats' poetry
✓ John Keats's poetry

Adding an -s, does, however, add a syllable to the word. The way place names are pronounced in their possessive form will indicate whether an extra -s is customarily added:

No extra -s   St Albans' town centre is always busy.
Extra -s   St James's Park closes at 9 p.m.

Note: Some expressions referring to time require a possessive apostrophe:

an hour's drive   (the drive of/for an hour)
a moment's thought   (the thought of a moment)
a day's work   (the work of a day)
ten months' time   (in the time of ten months)
fifteen years' imprisonment (imprisonment for fifteen years)

Do not use an apostrophe with words like hers, yours, ours, and theirs. The concept of ownership/possession is already built in:

✓ That is hers.
✓ Have you chosen yours?
✓ We've lost ours.
✓ My neighbours have lent me theirs.

Apostrophes of omission

Apostrophes are used in contractions (words that have been shortened by omitting letters):

They're off!	(They are off.)
It's not fair. ⎫	
It isn't fair. ⎭	(It is not fair.)
Breakfast's ready.	(Breakfast is ready.)
Who's there?	(Who is there?)

You will see that when two words are combined in a contraction, the apostrophe indicates the missing letters. Be particularly careful not to put the apostrophe in the wrong place in contractions involving 'not':

✓ didn't   (= did not)
✗ did'nt
✓ shouldn't   (= should not)
✗ should'nt

Most contractions are straightforward, but there are three slightly odd ones – at least, they are odd when you think about them:

aren't I?	(= am I not?)
won't	(= will not)
shan't	(= shall not)

These contracted forms are used whenever you want an easy, conversational style (in letters to friends, for example). In very formal writing, you should avoid contractions and write the constructions in full.

INVERTED COMMAS (ALSO KNOWN AS QUOTATION MARKS OR SPEECH MARKS)

Inverted commas, whether single (' ') or double (" "), are used around:

◆ quotations
◆ certain titles

♦ words that are being singled out
♦ direct speech.

Quotations

Inverted commas are used around quotations. (It doesn't matter whether you use single or double inverted commas, but be consistent.)

> The famous line 'Reader, I married him' begins the last chapter of the novel.
> The famous line "Reader, I married him" begins the last chapter of the novel.

Sometimes the quotation will come at the end of your sentence. Remember the end stop marks the end of the sentence as a whole and it will come after the inverted commas.

> She has been called 'the most beautiful woman in the world'.
> She has been called "the most beautiful woman in the world".

(This is not American English practice, however, which would place the end stop inside the inverted commas as in direct speech.)

Note: If the quotation itself ends with a question mark or exclamation mark, this will need to be included with the quotation, but a full stop will still be needed at the end of the sentence as a whole.

Titles

Inverted commas are used around titles of plays, novels, poems, films, television and radio programmes and names of newspapers and magazines etc. Use either single or double inverted commas.

> His butler presses his copy of 'The Times' every morning.
> Have you read "White Teeth"?
> The local drama group is performing "Who's Afraid of Virginia Woolf?".

If you wish, you can underline titles instead of enclosing them in inverted commas:

His butler presses his copy of <u>The Times</u> every morning.

In print, titles are usually italicised instead of being enclosed within inverted commas.

Words that are being singled out

Some examples will make this use clear. Single inverted commas are usually used:

The Treasurer objected to the use of the word 'dishonest'.
I am not 'into' antiques.
How do you spell 'separate'?
The word 'arrogant' describes his manner exactly.

Direct speech

Inverted commas are used around the words actually spoken in dialogue in a novel or short story or other account, and indicate where the speech begins and ends. (Either single or double inverted commas can be used but be consistent.)

"Will you marry me?" Colin whispered passionately.
Susan replied firmly, "Never! I shall never marry."
"Never?" he asked, recoiling a little. "Do you really mean that?"

In a play, the actual words spoken would be presented differently and kept very separate from the narrative:

Colin (passionately):	Will you marry me?
Susan (firmly):	Never! I shall never marry.
Colin:	Never? (recoiling a little) Do you really mean that?

Notice also how the correct punctuation of direct speech is further subject to conventions governing the use of capital letters and commas. Notice their use in these four basic patterns:

♦ Speech first, narrative second:
"We will be a few minutes late," she said apologetically.

♦ Narrative first, speech second:
She said apologetically, "We will be a few minutes late."

♦ Speech interrupted by narrative:
"We will," she said apologetically, "be a few minutes late."

♦ Two or more sentences of speech:
"We will be a few minutes late," she said apologetically. "Daniel rarely gets home before seven. You know what the traffic is like on the M25. We'll be with you as soon as we can."

Take a new line for each speaker in a dialogue. This makes it easier for the reader to follow the conversation:

"Of course, I understand," Muriel said.
"You do?"
"But, of course. I don't blame you at all."
"Sure?"
"Absolutely sure!"
"Well, that's a relief!" exclaimed Ellie.

Note: Inverted commas are used around direct speech (the words actually spoken) but are never used around indirect speech (a report of what was said):

Direct speech (use inverted commas):
"I don't want to go to the ball," she said.

Indirect speech (don't use inverted commas):
She said that she didn't want to go to the ball.

HYPHENS

Hyphens (-) are used in:

♦ word division
♦ compound words.

Word division

A hyphen at the end of a line indicates that the word is continued on the next.

It really is best not to divide a word in this way because there is a risk the reader will be confused. Words look unfamiliar when they are divided and if the words are divided unwisely, readers may be stopped temporarily dead in their tracks:

✗ Megan ran down the path and into her father's arms

If you must break a word, choose a break between syllables that doesn't distort the pronunciation. The reader can then start saying the word mentally at the end of one line and continue smoothly at the beginning of the next:

✓ On Wednesday evening, we all enjoyed Charles's dem-
onstration of how to take a cutting.
✗ On Wednesday evening, we all enjoyed Charles's demon-
stration of how to take a cutting. (Charles's demon...?)

Just one hyphen is needed (at the end of the first line) to indicate that the word is to be continued on the next. Avoid breaking words mid-syllable.

Compound words

Words can be combined with hyphens to make one word:

He gave me a devil-may-care grin.
She has a happy-go-lucky temperament.

See the difference in meaning the positioning of hyphens can make:

Jack placed twenty-two pound coins on the counter. (= £22)
Jack placed twenty two-pound coins on the counter. (= £40)

Some compound words can be problematical. Many words now written as one word were once written as two and then, in a period in between, were hyphenated. It can be difficult deciding which stage a word has reached. Consult your dictionary when in doubt.

DASHES

Dashes (–) are used to indicate:

◆ a dramatic pause
◆ hesitation
◆ an interpolation.

Dramatic pauses

Here are some examples:

All I can say is – get out!
She opened the front door and stood there – naked!

Hesitation

Dashes are useful devices for indicating unfinished or breathless sentences:

I wonder – oh, dear! – you must have guessed – it's not easy to explain – would you mind if – I don't know how to put this –

Interpolations

A pair of dashes can be used to separate an additional remark or comment from the main structure of the sentence:

And just as I reached the phone – wouldn't you know it? – it stopped ringing.

In the middle of my driving test – just my luck – the fan belt went.

Dashes used like this are very informal. You would use them in a letter to a friend but not in an important document. They capture a conversational tone.

BRACKETS

Brackets can be used (like a pair of commas and a pair of dashes) to separate additional information from the main structure of the sentence:

He was 39 years of age (although I did not know this at the time).

Use 350g (12oz) of peeled and chopped plum tomatoes.

Brackets separate the enclosed information more powerfully than a pair of dashes. Dashes in their turn are more powerful than commas:

The second candidate (a Cambridge graduate) was outstanding.

The second candidate – a Cambridge graduate – was outstanding.

The second candidate, a Cambridge graduate, was outstanding.

All three ways of punctuating this sentence are correct. Choose whichever suits your purpose best at the time and in context.

COLONS

The special function of the colon (:) is to introduce a list. Experienced readers know what to expect when they reach a colon in a sentence:

I'm taking just *the bare essentials*: a sleeping bag, a toothbrush and a torch.

Every time I try to reason with her, I make *the same mistakes*: I choose a bad time and place and lose my temper.

Notice how you always have a general 'summing up' word (or words) before the colon and the itemised list after it:

We've planted a range of vegetables: onions, carrots, runner beans, peas and tomatoes.

My husband has some marvellous qualities: he is loyal; he is honest; he is very hardworking; and he is very generous.

SEMICOLONS

The semicolon (;) has two distinct functions:

◆ It can join two or more sentences that are closely related in meaning.
◆ It can separate items in a list.

Joining sentences

The advantages of using a semicolon to join two or more sentences related in meaning are two-fold:

◆ short sentences are combined into what may be a more pleasing longer one

◆ the meaning is made subtly clearer because the semicolon emphasises the relationship between the statements it joins.

Here is an example of a semicolon joining two short sentences:

She feels very tired. She did not sleep well last night.
She feels very tired; she did not sleep well last night.

Here are some more examples. Note that to combine sentences with a semicolon is always optional. Moreover, it should only be done if it enhances the meaning by pointing to the connection between the sentences.

The marriage has come to an end. They were basically incompatible.
The marriage has come to an end; they were basically incompatible.

You are working very hard. You deserve to get good grades.
You are working very hard; you deserve to get good grades.

The donkey was in a pitiable state. It was very thin and clearly very ill.
The donkey was in a pitiable state; it was very thin and clearly very ill.

Replacing commas in a list

The second function of the semicolon is to separate items in a list instead of using the comma. Commas are probably better in a simple list with short items, but semicolons come into their own in a more complicated list where the items are described more fully in constructions requiring commas of their own:

He packed a pair of comfortable old sneakers, which he'd had for years; a pair of shorts, which he could wear for swimming as well as for walking; a couple of sweatshirts which had useful pockets; smart white trousers; and, last but not least, a brightly coloured cotton shirt, which he had bought in Miami.

Part Seven

◆ Spelling

9

Spelling

All of us need to check how to spell certain words from time to time but some people find spelling quite problematical. What can be done about it?

There are four major tactics that can be adopted:

- use a good dictionary
- use a spelling notebook
- know the basic spelling rules
- use memory aids.

DICTIONARY

A 'good' dictionary is one that meets your needs. The layout of dictionaries varies enormously. If you need to replace the one you have, spend some time in a well-stocked bookshop, looking carefully at the dictionaries there. A dictionary is, of course, multi-functional: it will help you with spelling, meaning, punctuation, and possibly usage and derivation. It is well worth looking up the same word in a number of dictionaries and seeing which presentation you find the most helpful.

There are specific spelling dictionaries which you may also decide to invest in. Look at some and see what you think. Some indicate common misspellings and guide you to the correct spelling:

> ✗ peticularly = particularly
> ✗ fionsay   = fiancé or fiancée
> ✗ apon   = upon

This can be very helpful if you are unsure of how the word begins. You usually need to know the first three letters to be able to locate a word in a regular dictionary. If you don't know the first three letters, it can be very frustrating.

A good dictionary is one that enables you to find the guidance you require as easily as possible.

SPELLING NOTEBOOK

You will find it helpful to collect the words you most frequently need to look up. Buy an indexed notebook and enter correct spellings alphabetically in this easily located source.

A notebook can fit in a pocket or handbag and can be with you at work as well as at home. You will probably find that it is a relatively small pool of words that is causing you trouble. The mere act of looking them up will help to reinforce the correct spelling. This will be a great boost to your confidence. You will be tackling positively the words that have hitherto caused you the most trouble.

SPELLING RULES

It is true that there are thousands of words in the English language that need to be learned by heart individually. But it is also true that there are thousands which do obey rules (or follow patterns). Observe these patterns. They are quite straightforward.

Rule 1
Most words form their plurals simply by adding -s:

book	s	crocodile	s
island	s	election	s
shop	s	pencil	s
examination	s	prawn	s
daughter	s	example	s
holiday	s	supermarket	s

Rule 2

Words which end in a sibilant (a hissing sound like -s, -x, -ch, -tch, -sh, -z) form their plurals by adding -es. This provides the extra syllable needed to make the word pronounceable. If you say these words aloud, you will hear the extra syllable:

address	es	church	es	brush	es
loss	es	porch	es	wish	es
iris	es	bench	es	blemish	es
atlas	es	inch	es	sash	es
prefix	es	match	es	waltz	es
hoax	es	watch	es		
fox	es	pitch	es		
lynx	es	witch	es		

*Some words double the final -z before adding -es:

fez (singular)
fezes or fezzes (plural)
quiz (singular)
quizzes (plural)

Check in a dictionary if in doubt.

Rule 3: Words ending in -y

The secret of applying this rule with success every time is to look at the letter which comes immediately before the final -y. Is it a vowel or a consonant?

Of the 26 letters of the alphabet, five are vowels: a e i o u. The rest are consonants.

Words ending in a vowel + y add -s to form the plural:

day	s	days
holiday	s	holidays
chimney	s	chimneys
pulley	s	pulleys
boy	s	boys
convoy	s	convoys
guy	s	guys

Words ending in a consonant + y change the y to i and add -es:

bab(y)	i	es	babies
lad(y)	i	es	ladies
butterfl(y)	i	es	butterflies
enem(y)	i	es	enemies
pupp(y)	i	es	puppies
soliloqu(y)	i	es	soliloquies
factor(y)	i	es	factories
fantas(y)	i	es	fantasies
cit(y)	i	es	cities
nav(y)	i	es	navies
galax(y)	i	es	galaxies

Note: the letters 'qu' count together as a consonant.

The only exceptions to this rule are the plurals of people's names, when -s is added every time to avoid distortion:

- ✓ The Hardys came to supper last night. (Mr and Mrs Hardy)
- ✓ There are three Maries in the class and five Marys.
  (= three called Marie and five called Mary)

Rule 4: Words ending in -o
Most words ending in -o form their plurals by simply adding -s:

piano	s		video	s
photo	s		tattoo	s
commando	s		poncho	s

A few plurals can be spelled either -os or -oes. Check in your dictionary for these. They include:

halos or haloes   innuendos or innuendoes
mementos or mementoes   mosquitos or mosquitoes

A few plurals have to be -oes. There aren't many of them but they include some high-frequency everyday words. It may be worth learning this short list by heart:

buffalo	es	cargo	es
echo	es	hero	es
potato	es	tomato	es
veto	es	volcano	es

Rule 5: Words ending in -f and -fe

Most words ending in -f or -fe add -s to form the plural:

roof	s	proof	s
belief	s	handkerchief	s
cliff	s	sheriff	s
giraffe	s	carafe	s

There are 13 exceptions to the rule. These end in -ves. You can always hear -ves when you say these words aloud:

calves	leaves	selves	thieves
elves	lives	sheaves	wives
halves	loaves	shelves	wolves
knives			

Four plurals can be either -fs or -ves. Use whichever you prefer but be prepared to see either in your reading.

hoofs or hooves   turfs or turves
scarfs or scarves   wharfs or wharves

These five rules for plurals are useful because they are the key to hundreds of words, and there are very few exceptions. Some other plurals in the English language, however, are quite irregular.

Always use your dictionary when in doubt as to how to form the plural of foreign words absorbed into the language (phenomenon becomes phenomena; synopsis becomes synopses; nebula becomes nebulae, and so on).

Some foreign words have two plurals, one foreign and one anglicised, sometimes with a difference in meaning, for example appendices and appendixes; indices and indexes.

Some words are identical in the singular and in the plural, for example deer, salmon, trout; others have no singular form, for example scissors, trousers, pliers. Fortunately, these are familiar words in common use and cause no difficulty to native English speakers, but imagine how puzzling foreign students must find some of our plurals, such as child – children, woman – women, tooth – teeth, goose – geese.

There are five more spelling rules that are well worth knowing:

Rule 6: The ie/ei rule

The rule in its entirety has very few exceptions. Unfortunately most people know the rule only in a garbled form. Here it is in full:

> Put i before e except after c
> Or when sounded like a
> As in 'neighbour' and 'weigh'.

Some ie words:

believe	priest	fierce	handkerchief
niece	achieve	diesel	grievance

Some ei words (after c):

receive	conceited	deceitful
ceiling	conceive	perceive

Some ei words (that sound like a):

neighbour	weigh	reign	rein
veil	eight	skein	vein

There are just a few exceptions, but not many:

either	forfeit	leisure	surfeit
neither	heifer	protein	their
counterfeit	heir	seize	weir
foreign	height	sovereign	weird

Also words where -ci- makes a 'sh' sound:

ancient	sufficient	efficient
proficient	deficient	*glacier (= 3 syllables)
conscience	species	

Note: Some names do not follow the rule either: Deirdre, Sheila, Keith, Neil, etc.

The remaining four rules are all concerned with adding suffixes (endings) to words. When do you drop the -e of the base word? When do you double the last letter? There are clear guidelines to hand! You don't have to guess.

Rule 7: The silent-e rule
It all depends on whether the suffix you are adding begins with a vowel or a consonant.

If the suffix begins with a consonant, keep the -e at the end of the base word:

care	ful	careful
care	less	careless
love	ly	lovely
state	ment	statement
white	ness	whiteness
some	thing	something
safe	ty	safety

If the suffix begins with a vowel, drop the -e:

admir(e)	able	admirable
ignor(e)	ance	ignorance
generat(e)	ion	generation
car(e)	ing	caring
behav(e)	iour	behaviour
fam(e)	ous	famous
laz(e)	y*	lazy

*y counts as a vowel when it sounds like i or e.

There are nine exceptions to the rule that you keep the -e before a consonant. In these words the -e is dropped:

truly	argument	width
duly	wholly	whilst
ninth	awful	wisdom

The sentence 'Truly and duly the ninth argument is wholly awful' may help you to remember them. Perhaps you can make up a sentence of your own. Only nine exceptions, and a rule that will help you to spell correctly thousands of words. It's a rule worth learning.

There are also a few exceptions to the rule that you drop the -e before a suffix beginning with a vowel. But there is a good reason for this:

◆ The -e is kept in words like:
pronounceable
noticeable
knowledgeable
manageable
courageous.

Note: The presence of the e keeps c soft as in 'centre' and g soft as in 'gentle'. Before a and o, both sounds are usually hard (cat, cot, gap, got).

◆ The e is vital in singe + ing (singeing) to distinguish it from sing + ing (singing) and in dye + ing (dyeing) to distinguish it from die + ing (dying).

◆ Some words like mileage, canoeing, hoeing keep the -e. Always check in a dictionary if in doubt.

◆ The -e is retained before consonant suffixes but note these alternative forms. Both are correct:
acknowledgement/acknowledgment
judgement/judgment.

Rule 8: The -y rule

When we were looking at the plural form of words ending in -y, we saw that it was vital to look at the letter that came immediately before the -y. The same is true with Rule 8.

If the word ends in a vowel + y, simply add the suffix:

play	er	player
play	ing	playing
play	ful	playful
employ	ee	employee
employ	ed	employed
employ	er	employer
employ	ment	employment

If the word ends in a consonant + y, change the y to i before adding the suffix:

appl(y)	i	ance	appliance
den(y)	i	al	denial
beaut(y)	i	ful	beautiful
empt(y)	i	ness	emptiness
stud(y)	i	ous	studious
penn(y)	i	less	penniless
fift(y)	i	eth	fiftieth
hungr(y)	i	ly	hungrily

If the suffix already begins with i-, you don't have to change the -y of the base word. (You don't want 'ii' in the middle of the word.)

try	ing	trying
apply	ing	applying
baby	ish	babyish

There are very few exceptions to the -y rule and so once again this is a really useful rule. The exceptions are as follows:

baby	babyhood
day	daily
dry	dryness (but drier, driest)
gay	gaily, gaiety
lay	laid (mislaid etc.)
pay	paid (repaid, prepaid etc.)
say	said
shy	shyness, shyly, shyer, shyest
slay	slain (but slayer)
sly	slyness, slyly/slily, slyer/slier, slyest/sliest
wry	wryness, wryly, wryer/wrier, wryest/wriest

Rule 9: The one-one-one rule
One-one-one words are so called because they are words of one syllable,

ending with one consonant preceded by one vowel. Words such as 'big', 'pin', 'stop' are one-one-one words.

There is no change to a one-one-one word before adding a suffix beginning with a consonant:

sin	ful	sinful
spot	less	spotless
drop	let	droplet
mad	ly	madly
sad	ness	sadness

Adding a suffix beginning with a vowel, however, needs care because you have to double the final letter of the base word:

sin	n	er	sinner
spot	t	ed	spotted
drop	p	ing	dropping
mad	d	en	madden
sad	d	er	sadder
sad	d	est	saddest

Exceptions: Simply this instruction: never double w, x, y before a vowel suffix. It would look very odd:

> stewed (not stewwed!)
> vexed (not vexxed!)
> stayed (not stayyed!)

Rule 10: The two-one-one rule

Two-one-one words are words of two syllables, ending with one consonant preceded by one vowel. Words such as 'limit', 'forget', 'tender', 'commit' are two-one-one words.

The key to this rule lies in the way the words are pronounced. You have to decide whether the first syllable is emphasised when you say the word aloud, or whether the second syllable is emphasised. This only matters when you are adding a vowel suffix (an ending beginning with a vowel).

There is no change to the base word before adding a consonant suffix:

forget	ful	forgetful
limit	less	limitless
commit	ment	commitment
tender	ness	tenderness

There is similarly no change to the base word before adding a vowel suffix if the stress falls on the first syllable of the base word: PROfit, ORbit ALter, GALLop, DIFFer, FASTen, GOSSip:

PRO fit	able	profitable
OR bit	al	orbital
AL ter	ation	alteration
GALL op	ed	galloped
DIFF er	ence	difference
FAST en	er	fastener
GOSS ip	ing	gossiping

However, double the final consonant of the base word before adding a vowel suffix if the stress fall on the second syllable: acQUIT, adMIT, abHOR, subMIT, beGIN, forGET:

ac QUIT	t	al	acquittal
ad MIT	t	ance	admittance
ab HOR	r	ence	abhorrence
sub MIT	t	ed	submitted
be GIN	n	er	beginner
for GET	t	ing	forgetting

There are a few exceptions:

◆ Words ending in -l are tricky. You'll probably do best to check them in a dictionary unless you can remember that you never double before -ity or -ise/ize (formality, legalise/legalize). And that you always double before any other vowel ending (excellent, cancellation, quarrelling, controller, etc.).

◆ These three words always double the final consonant before a vowel suffix: worship, kidnap, outfit.

◆ As with the one-one-one rule, never double final w, x, y – it would look very odd.

◆ There are just a few words where the stress changes on words within the same family. This is reflected in the spelling, depending on whether the stress is on the first or second syllable in the final form:

conFERRed	conFERRing	but	CONference
deFERRed	deFERRing	but	DEFerence
preFERRed	preFERRing	but	PREFerence
reFERRed	reFERRing	but	REFerence
transFERRed	transFERRing	but	TRANSference

MEMORY AIDS

Some words have to be learned by heart. There are various methods of memorising that may help you with 'stubborn' words.

Look carefully at the word

Learn to look carefully at words and try to break them into manageable units. Don't be frightened away by an unfamiliar word. If you look closely, you will probably find that most of the word is straightforward enough. Try to make up ways to help yourself remember the 'difficult' bits.

If you have trouble learning 'separate', for example, (it's usually the fourth letter that people get wrong), you may be helped by remembering there is 'a rat' in the middle of the word. Add 'sep' at the beginning and 'e' at the end and you'll never fear this word again (or words in the same family such as 'separation' and 'separately').

If the word is one such as 'Wednesday', try saying it aloud as three separate syllables = Wed nes day. This distorted pronunciation makes it straightforward to spell.

Make up mnemonics (memory aids) to help you with words you keep getting wrong at the same point:

idiosyncracy or idiosyncrasy? ✓ idiosyncraSy (Silly me!)
secertary or secretary?   ✓ Secretary
                                            (A SECRETary can keep a SECRET.)
iland or island?   ✓ island (There IS the island.)

Acronyms can be useful:

Rhythm = r + h + y + t + h + m:

(Rhythm Has Your Two Hips Moving.)

And remember:

> a stationARy cAR
> My NIce NIece NIcola
> My PAL the PrinciPAL

Use any mnemonics you come across that will help you, and make up your own. The more ridiculous they are, the more useful you will find them because you will remember them more easily.

Word families

As your confidence grows, you'll learn to make use of your knowledge of one word in a word family to help you with another. Look out for family characteristics. You will be helped to remember the silent letter 'g' in 'sign', for example, if you remember the spelling of 'signature', which is formed from it, and in which 'g' is pronounced quite clearly. Similarly you won't forget the 'n' in 'government' if you remember the 'n' at the end of 'govern'.

Derivation

Knowing about the derivation of words helps enormously not only with fully understanding their meaning but also with their spelling. For example, you will always remember how to spell 'desperate' if you know its derivation.

It comes from the Latin words *de* (= away) and *sperare* (= to hope). The tricky letter in 'desperate' is the fifth letter. You won't make a mistake if you think of *spErare*. Similarly if you know the word *beau* in French, then you already know how to spell the tricky first syllable of the English 'beautiful'.

Make use of what you already know. Draw upon your assets.

Part Eight

◆ Words that are often confused

10

Words That Are Often Confused

Some of the pairs of words that are most often confused are listed below. Grammatical terms like 'noun' and 'verb' have not been used as they are not helpful to readers unfamiliar with them. Instead, meanings are given and examples of the words in use. You should be able to 'match up' your requirement from this when you are unsure.

accept/except

◆ accept = to agree or be willing to receive
I accept your invitation with great pleasure.
They accepted the lowest offer in the end.
The young thug was found guilty and will have to accept the consequences.

◆ except = leaving out, not including
Everyone came to the party except James.
She liked all the designs except this one.

advice/advise

◆ advice = suggestions about what should be done
Take my advice and leave him.
Eleanor decided to seek professional advice.

◆ advise = to make suggestions about what should be done
I advised her to leave him.
What would you advise me to do?

affect/effect

◆ affect = to influence
Michael's sudden death affected all who knew him.

Ice and snow would <u>affect</u> our plans, but nothing else.

Does wet weather <u>affect</u> your arthritis?

◆ effect = result, impact, working state

The <u>effect</u> of the new medicine was dramatic.

Your tears have no <u>effect</u> on me.

The new law comes into <u>effect</u> next Monday.

effect = to make something happen, to bring about

The moment he became Managing Director, he began to <u>effect</u> changes.

allowed/aloud

◆ allowed = permitted

Are we <u>allowed</u> to smoke here?

Her children are never <u>allowed</u> to go out alone.

◆ aloud = out loud

Read this poem <u>aloud</u> with as much expression as you can.

alternate/alternative

◆ alternate = every other one (pronounced al-TERN-ate)

The club meets on <u>alternate</u> Mondays.

alternate = to take turns (pronounced AL-tern-ate)

My friend and I <u>alternate</u> our day off. It's like a job share really.

◆ alternative = a choice (usually between two possibilities)

The <u>alternatives</u> are simple: work or go hungry.

We really had no <u>alternative</u> but to accept his offer.

alternative = giving a choice

An <u>alternative</u> plan would be to fly rather than take the train.

The Royal Family have always been interested in <u>alternative</u> medicine.

among/between

'Among' refers to more than two; 'between' generally refers to two people, things, possibilities, etc.

You are <u>among</u> friends here.

Discuss it <u>among</u> yourselves.

<u>Between</u> you and me, he's totally unreliable.

I really can't choose <u>between</u> them. They're both lovely.

Emily divides her time <u>between</u> her two houses.

Note, however, that 'between' is sometimes used with more than two:

It will take a long time before the differences <u>between</u> the five parties concerned are resolved.

as/like

◆ as

Dermot cannot come with us <u>as</u> he's totally exhausted.

You look <u>as</u> if you've seen a ghost.

<u>As</u> they promised, they've settled all their bills on time.

◆ like

She looks just <u>like</u> her sister.

bath/bathe

◆ bath = to wash oneself or to wash someone else in a bath
Some people like to <u>bath</u> in the morning; some prefer evenings.
Dermot is <u>bathing</u> the baby.

◆ bathe = to swim
Josephine <u>bathes</u> in the Atlantic, every day, rain or shine.

bathe = to cover with water, to cleanse
We were advised to <u>bathe</u> the wound twice a day.
Julia gazed out of the window, her face <u>bathed</u> in tears.

between (see among/between)

board/bored

◆ board = a flat piece of wood

My parents have decided to sand and polish the floor<u>board</u>s.
The advertisement was stolen from the notice<u>board</u>.

◆ bored = not interested
Everybody shuffled and looked <u>bored</u> as the speaker droned on and on.

borrow/lend

◆ borrow = to take something temporarily (usually with the owner's permission), intending to return it later.
May I <u>borrow</u> your car while mine is being serviced?

◆ lend = to give something to someone on a temporary basis, expecting it to be returned.
He wanted me to <u>lend</u> him my car. I had to refuse.

bought/brought

◆ bought = the past tense of 'to buy'
I <u>bought</u> enough food to feed an army. It cost a fortune.

◆ brought = the past tense of 'to bring'
The children <u>brought</u> their swimming things with them just in case there was a chance of going to the beach.

buy/by

◆ buy = to purchase
We want to <u>buy</u> you a special present.

◆ by
Wait <u>by</u> the car.
The play is <u>by</u> Oscar Wilde.
They ran <u>by</u>, without speaking.

coarse/course

◆ coarse = rough, vulgar, offensive
His jacket was made of a <u>coarse</u> material.
When Sean has had too much to drink, his language becomes very <u>coarse</u>.

◆ course = direction, series (especially of lessons), one of the parts of a meal

The ship was blown off course in the gale.

Marie has enrolled on a wine-tasting course.

He's almost finished the course of injections now.

For our main course, we're having roast duck and red cabbage.

of course = certainly

Of course, I'd love to come to your party!

clothes/cloths

◆ clothes = garments

When I've lost another stone, I shall need some new clothes.

◆ cloths = pieces of fabric (used for housework etc.)

Have you any old cloths I can use for cleaning my bike?

complement/compliment

◆ complement = the full amount needed (that which completes)

The ship has its full complement of crew now.

complement = to go well with

That blue scarf complements your blue eyes perfectly.

◆ compliment = words of praise

Matthew paid me the nicest compliment I've ever received when he said I always cheered him up.

compliment = to pay someone a compliment

I complimented her afterwards for having kept her temper.

compose of/comprise

◆ compose of

The audience was composed of parents, and children under ten years of age.

◆ comprise

The audience comprised parents, and children under ten years of age.

continual/continuous

◆ continual = repeated with breaks, recurring
I cannot cope with these <u>continual</u> interruptions and silly remarks.

◆ continuous = continuing without stopping
The noise from the motorway is <u>continuous</u> both day and night. It never stops.

councillor/counsellor

◆ councillor = an elected member of a council. (Usually abbreviated to Cllr.)
<u>Cllr</u>. Roberts is a very hard-working member of the Planning Committee.

◆ counsellor = an adviser, one who counsels
The student was helped greatly by the Study <u>Counsellor</u>.
Teresa is training to be a Marriage <u>Counsellor</u>.

disinterested/uninterested

◆ disinterested = having no selfish motive, not standing to gain
His motives were entirely <u>disinterested</u>. He just wanted to help.

◆ uninterested = bored, not interested
She's completely <u>uninterested</u> in sport or any physical activity, and yet I wouldn't call her lazy.

drawers/draws

◆ drawers = old-fashioned knickers, sliding containers in a piece of furniture
Do you remember those lisle stockings and baggy <u>drawers</u> women used to wear?
Helen's bought a beautiful mahogany chest of <u>drawers</u> in a house auction.

◆ draws (from 'to draw')
Toby <u>draws</u> beautifully. He's very artistic.
I'm always taken by surprise at that point in the play when he <u>draws</u> his sword.

effect (see affect/effect)

except (see accept/except)

fewer/less

◆ fewer = not so many
There are <u>fewer</u> poppies in cornfields nowadays.
<u>Fewer</u> sparrows are seen in town gardens.

◆ less = not so much
I have <u>less</u> enthusiasm for walking these days.
We all eat <u>less</u> than the Victorian middle classes used to eat.

heard/herd

◆ heard = the past tense of 'to hear'
I thought I <u>heard</u> a noise downstairs but there was no one there.

◆ herd = a collective term for cows, elephants, etc.
My way was blocked by a <u>herd</u> of cows, ambling very slowly along the lane.

hole/whole

◆ hole = an opening in something
Did you know that you have a <u>hole</u> in your sock?

◆ whole = entire
Sharon ate the <u>whole</u> packet of biscuits by herself.

imply/infer

◆ imply = to hint, to suggest subtly
Jake felt that the lecturer was <u>implying</u> that he had cheated but he didn't accuse him in so many words.

◆ infer = to draw a conclusion from the evidence
The detective <u>inferred</u> that it had been raining at the time of entry. There were muddy footprints all across the carpet.

its/it's

◆ its = belonging to it
That book has lost <u>its</u> dustjacket.
The dog wagged <u>its</u> tail.
My chewing-gum has lost <u>its</u> flavour. Has yours?

◆ it's = it is, it has
<u>It's</u> a pity we can't meet in Manchester. (= it is)
<u>It's</u> been raining all day.   (= it has)

know/no

◆ know = to understand, to be acquainted with, to have learnt
I <u>know</u> how you feel.
Do you <u>know</u> my parents?
James <u>knows</u> the French word for 'breakfast'.

◆ no = not any, opposite of 'yes'
Sheila has <u>no</u> doubts at all.
<u>No</u>, I'm afraid I can't help you.

lay/lie

◆ lay = to put something down, to prepare, to produce (eggs)
I <u>lay</u> the table each evening. } present tense
Hens <u>lay</u> eggs. }
I <u>laid</u> the table yesterday. } past tense
Her hens <u>laid</u> eggs yesterday. }

◆ lie = to rest in a horizontal position
I <u>lie</u> down every afternoon for an hour. (present tense)
I <u>lay</u> down yesterday afternoon but I couldn't sleep. (past tense)

lie = to tell an untruth
I <u>lie</u> whenever anyone asks how much I earn. (present tense)
I <u>lied</u> whenever anyone asked me how much I earned. (past tense)

learn/teach

◆ learn = to acquire knowledge
Rosemary is going to <u>learn</u> to drive this autumn.

◆ <u>teach</u> = to impart knowledge
My brother has promised to <u>teach</u> me to swim.

lend (see borrow/lend)

lie (see lay/lie)

like (see as/like)

loose/lose

◆ loose = not tight, not firm, easily removed (rhymes with 'noose')
Megan's front tooth is <u>loose</u>.
We're going to invest in <u>loose</u> covers for the old suite.

◆ lose = to mislay (rhymes with 'choose')
It's easy to <u>lose</u> your way in the dark.

meat/meet

◆ meat = the flesh of animals when used as food
Adrian won't eat <u>meat</u>: he's a vegetarian.

◆ meet = to encounter, to come face to face with
I'll <u>meet</u> you outside the cinema at 7.30 p.m.

no (see know/no)

of/off

◆ of (pronounced 'ov')
You've come top <u>of</u> the class. Congratulations!

◆ off (rhymes with 'scoff')
Get <u>off</u> now!

official/officious

◆ official = approved by a person in authority
This is an <u>official</u> warning. Next time you will be prosecuted.

◆ officious = fussy, self-important, interfering, telling you what to do in an annoying way, holding too rigidly to rules and regulations

Kevin pulled up at the entrance to the Casualty Department only to be waved on by an <u>officious</u> car-park attendant.

passed/past

♦ passed = past tense of 'to pass'
Jane <u>passed</u> his flat every day on the way to school.
The old man <u>passed</u> the form to the official.

♦ past
The waiter walked straight <u>past</u> my table.
He walked <u>past</u>.

past = opposite of 'the future'
In the <u>past</u>, things were done differently.
<u>Past</u> customs are always fascinating.

personal/personnel

♦ personal = belonging to or directed at a particular person
You don't have to give <u>personal</u> details if you don't want to.
I resented his remarks; they were very <u>personal</u> and rather insulting.

♦ personnel = all the people employed in an organisation
All the <u>personnel</u> have received computer training.
Write to the <u>Personnel</u> Officer and see if there's a vacancy.
I believe <u>Personnel</u> Officers are called Human Resources Managers now.

practice/practise

♦ practice = the business of a professional person, the doing of something so many times that you get better at it
His uncle has a dental <u>practice</u> in town.
<u>Practice</u> makes perfect.

♦ practise = to work at a profession, to do something so many times that you get better at it
His ambition has always been to <u>practise</u> as a dentist.
If you <u>practise</u> every day, you will get better at it.

precede/proceed

- precede = to go in advance, to go in front
  The Queen <u>precedes</u> her husband on official occasions.

- proceed = to carry on, especially after having stopped
  After threatening us all with violence, the highwayman <u>proceeded</u> to strip us of our jewellery.

principal/principle

- principal = chief, first in importance
  My <u>principal</u> objection is that it will deter students from poorer homes from applying.

  Principal = chief lecturer, someone in charge of a school or college
  The <u>Principal</u>, Dr Carey, introduced the main speaker at the graduation ceremony.

- principle = a rule, a truth, a belief that serves as a guide
  Mary-Jo has very strong <u>principles</u>; she would never betray a friend.

quiet/quite

- quiet = not noisy (qui - et = two syllables)
  Let's have a <u>quiet</u> evening tonight, just by ourselves.

- quite = entirely, fairly
  I'm <u>quite</u> exhausted.
  It's <u>quite</u> cold today.

raise/rise

- raise = to move something to a higher position, to collect, to introduce
  We've had to <u>raise</u> the roof by a metre to qualify for an improvement grant.
  The scouts have <u>raised</u> £300.
  Mike Pendlebury <u>raised</u> several objections at the meeting.

- rise = to get up, to become louder, to swell up, to move to a higher position
  My husband <u>rises</u> regularly at 7 a.m.
  The teacher's voice <u>rose</u> above the hubbub of voices.

Yeast helps the dough to <u>rise</u>.
My grandfather <u>rose</u> through the ranks to become a captain.

rise = an increase in pay
Simon asked for a <u>rise</u> but he didn't get it.

seam/seem

♦ seam = a stitched joining of two pieces of material, a thin layer in rock
We learned to sew a French <u>seam</u> at school in needlework classes.
The coal <u>seam</u> is now exhausted, but it yielded thousands of tons of coal in its time.

♦ seem = to appear
It would <u>seem</u> that we have no chance of getting the contract.
You <u>seem</u> very calm.

stationary/stationery

♦ stationary = not moving
The cyclist crashed into the <u>stationary</u> car.

♦ stationery = notepaper
<u>Stationery</u> is usually a welcome Christmas present for anyone who likes writing letters.

thank you/thank-you

♦ thank you
<u>Thank you</u> very much for your generous contribution.
May I say a huge '<u>thank you</u>'!

♦ thank-you
We wrote our <u>thank-you</u> letters on Boxing Day.

their/there/they're

♦ their = belonging to them
They have lost <u>their</u> puppy.

♦ there (there is/there are)
<u>There</u> is a rumour that he has left the country.

<u>There</u> are several clues.

+ there (indicating place)
Wait for me over <u>there</u> by the statue.
I'd love to go <u>there</u> one day.

+ they're = they are
<u>They're</u> hoping that insurance will cover it.
You know what <u>they're</u> like!

threw/through

+ threw = past tense of 'to throw'
Justin <u>threw</u> the ball further than anyone else.

+ through
Can you climb <u>through</u> the gap in the fence?
Read <u>through</u> the report carefully and tell me what you think.

to/too/two

+ to
The twins hope <u>to stay</u> in the same class.
We plan <u>to go</u> in the summer.
Try <u>to eat</u> a little.

Give that knife <u>to</u> me immediately.
Damien gave a present <u>to</u> his teacher.
His father's gone <u>to</u> London.
Shall we go <u>to</u> the cinema?

+ too = excessively
I know that I'm <u>too</u> fat.
I eat <u>too</u> much.
You're <u>too</u> generous.
<u>Too</u> many cooks spoil the broth.

too = as well
Harry is coming <u>too</u>.

+ two

They have <u>two</u> dogs, both Alsatians.
<u>Two</u> and <u>two</u> make four.

uninterested (see disinterested/uninterested)

weather/whether

* weather = climate
  Have you heard the <u>weather</u> forecast for the weekend?

* whether = if
  Sam doesn't know <u>whether</u> he can come with us to Paris.

were/where

* were = past tense of 'are'
  You <u>were</u> in a good mood last night.

* where (refers to 'place' like <u>h</u>ere, t<u>h</u>ere)
  <u>Where</u> are you?
  <u>Where</u> is my shirt?
  That's the house <u>where</u> I was born.
  They had no idea <u>where</u> they were.

whole (see hole/whole)

who's/whose

* who's = who is/who has
  <u>Who's</u> coming clubbing tonight?
  <u>Who's</u> been eating my porridge?
  There's the boy <u>who's</u> a genius at science.
  There's the woman <u>who's</u> won the lotto three times.

* whose = belonging to whom
  <u>Whose</u> earrings are these?
  <u>Whose</u> voice can I hear?
  My mother knows the man <u>whose</u> wife was killed in the accident.

The writer <u>whose</u> books you admire is my uncle.

your/you're

♦ your = belonging to you
Is this <u>your</u> coat?
<u>Your</u> husband is on the phone.

♦ you're = you are
I know <u>you're</u> not serious.
<u>You're</u> very kind.

Part Nine

◆ Useful spellings

11

Useful Spellings

absence
absent
absolutely
accidental
accidentally
accommodation
achievement
across
address
advertisement
aerial
afraid
aggressive
alcohol
all right
also
always
amateur
among
annoyed
annual
annually
anxiety
anxious
apologise (-ize)
apology
appalling

approached
argument
arrangements
assistant
athletics
attach
attached
attention
available
awkward

bachelor
beautiful
beginning
behaviour
believe
benefited
bicycle
Britain
broken
burglar
business

career
careful
carefully
careless

century
character
chief
chocolate
choice
circumstances
collapse
colleague
college
colossal
coming
comment
committee
comparative
comparison
completely
conscientious
convenient
criticise (-ize)
criticism

damage
decided
decision
definite
describe
description

despair	favourite	innocent
desperate	February	inoculate
detached	finally	insult
different	finish	intelligent
difficult	flexible	intention
dilapidated	foreign	interested
dining	formal	interrupt
disappear	formally	interview
disappoint	fortunately	intimidating
discuss	forty	irrelevant
disease	fourth	irritable
dissatisfied	friend	
	frightened	jealous
earnest	front	
eighth	further	knowledge
embarrass		
emergency	gauge	language
enthusiasm	government	leisure
environment	gradually	liaison
equipment	grateful	library
eventually	guarantee	likely
exaggerate	guard	literature
excellent	guidance	loneliness
excited		lonely
exercise	handkerchief	lovely
exhausted	harass	luxury
expect	honest	
expensive	humorous	maintain
experience	hygiene	maintenance
explanation		manager
extraordinary	immediately	managing director
extremely	immensely	marriage
	impossible	mathematics
familiar	indispensable	meant
family	information	medicine

menace

mention

millennium

miniature

mischievous

moment

mortgage

murmur

necessary

neighbour

nephew

niece

ninety

ninth

noticeable

nuisance

occasionally

occur

occurred

occurrence

omit

opinion

opportunity

originally

paid

parent

Parliament

perhaps

period

permanent

perseverance

persevere

persuade

pleasant

pleasure

possessions

possible

practically

prejudice

present

privilege

probably

professional

pronounce

pronunciation

qualification

quarter

questionnaire

queue

realise (-ize)

really

reasonable

receipt

receive

recent

recipe

recommend

referee

reference

refrigerator

regret

regrettably

regularly

relevant

repetition

resign

resignation

resources

responsibility

restaurant

ridiculous

rhyme

rhythm

sacrifice

safety

salary

sandwich

satellite

Saturday

scarcely

scheme

secretary

seize

sentence

separate

severely

shining

similar

sincerely

situation

something

sometimes

speak

specially

speech

success

successful

successfully

suggest

supersede

supervisor

support

suppose
surely
surprise
systematic
systematically

technical
temperature
temporarily
temporary
tendency
tired
tomorrow
tragedy
tragic
tried
truly

Tuesday
twelfth
typical

umbrella
unconscious
until
unusual
unusually
upon
useful
usual
usually

valuable
vegetable
vehicle

veterinary
view
virtually
visible
vocabulary
voluntarily
volunteer

Wednesday
weird
woman
women
woollen
writer
writing

Spell Well

Boost your word power and your confidence

Marion Field

' ... text is illustrated with a wealth of examples and there are two particularly interesting chapters on American spelling and new words, jargon and slang.'
– lsagency.org.uk

ISBN 978-1-84528-069-7

Read Faster, Recall More

Use proven techniques for speed reading and maximum recall

Gordon Wainwright

In today's information laden world, time is valuable. Reports, reference books, contracts, correspondence, newspapers, magazines and journals are just some of the things you might need to read and digest on a daily basis.

If you feel that the speed at which you read these items and the extent to which you are able to retain their information could be improved, then the use of the practical tips, proven techniques and numerous practise exercises in this book could help you to reach your potential. With the aid of this invaluable book, you can save time and achieve more.

' ... will help you to reduce the time spent on reading and recalling information.'
– *Evening Standard*

' ... purely practical and aims to help you in the professional environment.'
– *The Times*

'A worthwhile investment.' – *The Guardian*

ISBN 978-1-84528-162-5

Improve Your Punctuation and Grammar

Master the essentials of the English language and write with greater confidence

Marion Field

'An invaluable guide ... after reading this book, you will never again find yourself using a comma instead of a semi-colon.' – *London Evening Standard*

'I realised for the first time that grammar is actually fascinating ... you are given the facts in plain English – no waffle, no padding, just the details you really need ... a fascinating and readable book.' – *Writing Magazine*

'This book does exactly what it says on the front cover: it helps you master the basics of the English language and write with greater confidence and clarity.' – *MS London*

ISBN 978-1-85703-329-2

Quick Solutions to Common Errors in English

An A–Z guide to spelling, punctuation and grammar

Angela Burt

'You will never doubt your written English again.' – *Evening Standard*

'A very useful tool ... could easily fill that hole on your bookshelf.' – *Irish Independent*

' ... straightforward and accessible handbook for anyone who ever has a query about correct English – and that's all of us.' – *Freelance News*

ISBN 978-1-85703-947-4

Improve Your Written English

Master the essentials of grammar, punctuation and spelling and write with greater confidence

Marion Field

'If your written English is letting you down, do something about it. This book is recommended.' – *Evening Standard*

'This book is a gem. If you never buy another reference book, buy this one!' – *Writers' Express*

ISBN 978-1-85703-848-4

How to Pass Exams Every Time

Proven techniques for any exam that will boost your confidence and guarantee success

Mike Evans

Reading this book really will make a huge difference to exam performance, whatever exams you're taking. It isn't just hard work and intelligence that gets you through. In fact many hard working, intelligent people fail through lack of confidence or poor exam technique. At least 50 per cent of your chances are down to: your attitude to exams; the way you approach the course of study; and simple but effective techniques to use in the exam itself. These techniques are your guarantee of success – and what's more they're easy to learn and proven beyond doubt!

'Brisk, shrewd and full of useful tips.' – *Daily Telegraph*

ISBN 978-1-85703-933-7

How To Pay Less for More

The Consumer's Guide to Negotiating the Best Deals – Whatever You're Buying

'This book could save you thousands!'

Marc Lockley

This book will give you the skills to negotiate better deals in every area of your life. Marc Lockley, Negotiation Coach, teaches the basic negotiation skills and applies them to common situations that we all experience, either at home or in the workplace: buying a car, buying or selling a house, booking a holiday, planning a wedding or party, buying electrical goods, buying and fitting kitchens and bathrooms, complaining effectively and negotiating a pay rise or flexible hours. Marc estimates that by using the skills he teaches he saves himself thousands of pounds each year and has a higher standard of living than he might otherwise expect.

ISBN 978-1-84528-237-0

How To Get Good Care Services

for yourself or your relatives

Clare Kirkman

Care services are expanding and more organisations are opening, providing a better range of choice. Greater competition is pushing up standards of service and bringing better value-for-money. The tighter regulation of care services and improved quality control methods are increasing the power of consumers. As a modern consumer of care services you must take control of the process, whether the care is for you or for a loved one. This book explains where you can find care services and how to recognise quality care when you find it. It explains what you can expect in terms of the standard of care and service; and what you can do if you don't get it.

ISBN 978-1-84528-243-1

How to feed your whole family a healthy, balanced diet, with very little money and hardly any time, even if you have a tiny kitchen, only three saucepans (one with an ill-fitting lid) and no fancy gadgets – unless you count the garlic crusher ...

Simple, wholesome and nutritious recipes for family meals

Gill Holcombe

This book provides simple, wholesome and nutritious recipes for family meals; quick lunches, tasty puddings and cakes – and you don't have to spend hours slaving over a hot stove, or spend a fortune at the supermarket. There are menu plans, recipes, shortcuts and dozens of ideas for every meal, together with tried and tested tips to help you save your valuable time and money. Gill Holcombe is passionate about feeding her kids good food. She grew up before the culture of convenience food took hold – and knows how to cook. Having brought up three children on her own for over ten years, she says the proof of the pudding is in the eating, and has three fit, healthy teenagers with loads of energy – and no fillings in their teeth.

ISBN 978-1-905862-15-3

The Parent's Guide to Childcare

How to choose the right childcare for you and your child

Allison Lee

This book looks at the most popular types of childcare available and weighs up the advantages and disadvantages of each to help you to decide which service suits you best. It will help you to decide what kind of childcare you require; ensure that the relationship between the child and the carer and you and the carer work well; know what to expect from your childminder in terms of play and educational activities; know what to do when either your child or the carer is ill; understand the childcare contract and know what to do when things go wrong.

ISBN 978-1-84528-220-2

How To Books are available through all good bookshops, or you can order direct from us through Grantham Book Services.

Tel: +44 (0)1476 541080
Fax: +44 (0)1476 541061
Email: *orders@gbs.tbs-ltd.co.uk*

Or via our website

www.howtobooks.co.uk

To order via any of these methods please quote the title(s) of the book(s) and your credit card number together with its expiry date.

For further information about our books and catalogue, please contact:

How To Books
Spring Hill House
Spring Hill Road
Begbroke
Oxford
OX5 1RX

Visit our web site at

www.howtobooks.co.uk

Or you can contact us by email at info@howtobooks.co.uk